# MONTREALCOOKS

## RECIPES FROM MONTREAL'S FINEST RESTAURANTS

MUHC
McGILL UNIVERSITY HEALTH CENTRE
FOUNDATION

Women's
Health
MISSION

# MONTREALCOOKS
## RECIPES FROM MONTREAL'S FINEST RESTAURANTS

Chairperson & Editor-in-Chief
Karen Dubrofsky

Assistant Editors
Heidi Gossack-Majnemer, Donna Rabinovitch

Photography
Fahri Yavuz
www.yavuzphoto.com

Nutritional Analysis
Janis Morelli, Ann Coughlin

Creative Director
Cassi Design/Julie Siciliano
www.cassidesign.com

Layout & Graphic Design
Cassi Design/ Julie Siciliano & Maria Masella

Copy Editing & Proofreading
Knockout Communications

Translator & French Copy Editor
Marie Gouin, C.Tr.

Food Testers
Karen Dubrofsky, Julie Siciliano, Donna Rabinovitch, Heidi Gossack-Majnemer, Maria Masella

Advertising and Sponsorship
Karen Dubrofsky, the MUHC Foundation

For information about custom editions, special sales or premium or corporate purchases, please contact the MUHC Foundation at 514-931-5656 or online at **www.muhcfoundation.com**.

Copyright © 2007 MUHC Foundation

ISBN 978-0-9783843-0-2

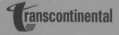

Printed in Canada by Transcontinental

**A NOTE TO COOKS:** *Montreal Cooks* is a labor of love, created through a collaboration between Montreal's finest chefs and our dedicated volunteers. Although every effort was made to ensure an accurate translation from the chefs' imaginations to these pages, we hope you will forgive any omissions or errors. Also note that the photographs are included for inspiration and reference, and may differ in presentation from the recipes as written.

On behalf of the McGill University Health Centre (MUHC) Foundation, thank you for purchasing *Montreal Cooks* and for supporting cancer care at the Women's Health Mission of the MUHC.

*Montreal Cooks* is truly a philanthropic "recipe for success": that ideal mix that comes when committed volunteers bring their creativity and talent to a cause they are passionate about. As we at the MUHC Foundation work to support the McGill University Health Centre in its mission to provide our community with the very best patient care, teaching and medical research, we cannot succeed without the support and involvement of our community. To find out how you can donate, volunteer or get involved with the MUHC Foundation and the *Best Care for Life* campaign, visit our website at **www.muhcfoundation.com**.

Once again, thank you for your support, and bon appetit…

*Montreal Cooks* represents the fulfillment of a long-time dream. As an avid cook and food aficionado, I have always appreciated the unlimited choices and international standard of cuisine offered by Montreal's many brilliant chefs. The opportunity to visit those chefs in their own kitchens, to explore some of their signature recipes, and then to share those recipes with others who have a passion for food seemed almost too good to be true.

At the same time, I envisioned this cookbook as a way to meaningfully contribute to a cause that is dear to my heart: the treatment of women suffering from cancer. My hope is that the sale of this book will allow us to achieve our goal of making a significant financial donation to the Women's Health Mission of the McGill University Health Centre. All the proceeds will go towards purchasing new equipment to improve the quality of care that the MUHC's talented and dedicated caregivers provide to women.

A lot of time and effort went into putting this cookbook together, yet none of it would have been possible without the involvement of a number of exceptional collaborators. First and foremost, I must thank the great chefs of our city, who overwhelmingly and positively responded to our idea. They shared their unique recipes with us and warmly welcomed us into their kitchens. It was with such enjoyment that I met these extraordinary professionals, watched them cook and witnessed their long hours of hard work and the true dedication they have for their craft.

This book also benefited from the help of two fantastic friends and fellow volunteers, Heidi Gossack-Majnemer and Donna Rabinovitch. My heartfelt thanks to these committed women for all their time, good humor and valuable input.

I would also like to extend a very sincere thank you to our photographer extraordinaire, Farhi Yavuz, and to our creative director Julie Siciliano and Flano Castelli from Cassi Design. Their talents are abundantly displayed throughout the beautiful pages of this book, but less visible is the generosity that motivated all three of them to give so many additional hours to its creation.

I am grateful to Janis Morelli and Ann Coughlin from the MUHC's Department of Clinical Nutrition, who enthusiastically provided a nutritional analysis of each recipe. I want to express sincere appreciation to Don Taddeo of the MUHC Foundation, to his helpful staff, especially Cindy Collin, Dianne Fagan and Yuri Mytko, and to Ronald Veilleux, who passed away due to cancer as this project was taking shape. His ideas and work at the onset helped us tremendously. Also, I would like to extend a special thank you to the team at the MUHC's Offices of Project Management, Technical Services and Planning for their efforts in support of this book.

On a personal note, an enormous thank you to my husband Lionel and my children Andrew, Lisa and Philip for putting up with the many, many hours I spent working on this book to its completion. I love all of you very much.

Finally, thank you to all our readers for your contribution. Not only will you be able to bring the tastes of Montreal's most glamorous restaurants into your own kitchen, you will, I hope, share my pride in knowing that you are supporting an important cause.

This cookbook has taught me that the key to delicious cooking is to use the freshest ingredients possible, to cook with passion and imagination, and to have a terrific recipe to follow. I trust that you will find that *Montreal Cooks* inspires you as much as creating it inspired me.

Karen Korzinstone Dubrofsky
Creator of *Montreal Cooks*

chairperson

editor-in-chief

As clinical nutritionists at the McGill University Health Centre, we help patients and caregivers understand the relationship between diet and their medical condition. We also teach them about making suitable food choices tailored to their individual needs. Therefore, the opportunity to provide nutritional analyses for the gorgeous collection of gourmet recipes found in *Montreal Cooks* was a novel diversion that we welcomed with both excitement and enthusiasm.

As we often tell our patients, eating well means enjoying a wide and balanced variety of foods, preparing meals with reasonable portions, emphasizing fresh ingredients, and most of all, taking pleasure in the act of eating, especially while in the company of good friends or family. The talented chefs who have shared their culinary creations in *Montreal Cooks* also share these ideals, and have provided recipes that can be included in a healthy diet. While some recipes are suitable for every day, others are best saved for those indulgent special occasions. In either case, it is our hope that the analyses will help you make informed choices as you incorporate these epicurean delights into your repertoire of sensational meals.

Enjoy!

Janis Morelli
Manager of Clinical Nutrition Services
Clinical Nutrition Services - Adult Sites

Ann Coughlin
Assistant Department Head
Clinical Nutrition Services - Adult Sites

As co-chairs of the Women's Health Committee of the *Best Care for Life* campaign, we want to express our sincere gratitude to Karen, Heidi and Donna for their creativity, commitment and tireless energy in putting together *Montreal Cooks*, and for generously dedicating the proceeds of this labor of love to oncology at the MUHC's Women's Health Mission.

As part of the $300-million *Best Care for Life* campaign in support of the MUHC's redevelopment, we are working to help raise the $15 million that has been dedicated to the current and future needs of the Women's Health Mission. This is an ambitious total, but one that we know the thousands of women cared for by the MUHC's devoted professionals both need and richly deserve.

Projects like *Montreal Cooks* inspire and encourage us as we work to help the MUHC provide the best care possible to women and their families. This book is truly a celebration of life and health, and we invite you to raise a glass to the Women's Health Mission as you enjoy these delectable recipes.

Maryse Bertrand
Co-Chair, Women's Health Committee

Pierrette Wong
Co-Chair, Women's Health Committee

As one of the seven core missions of the McGill University Health Centre, Women's Health holds pride of place in our institution. As research increasingly demonstrates, women have distinct health needs that require a new approach to care: one that focuses not only on excellence in reproductive medicine, but on the specific symptoms and treatments that women require for everything from cardiovascular disease to osteoporosis, depression and cancer. At the MUHC, we are one of the few institutions in Canada to offer an integrated and multidisciplinary approach to the full gamut of Women's Health services, providing sensitive and innovative care to women at every stage of their lives.

As we work to provide the best care for women today and as we move closer to the completion of our redeveloped facilities at the MUHC's new Glen and Mountain campuses, it is heartening to receive the support of exceptional volunteers like Karen Dubrofsky and her collaborators. *Montreal Cooks* is a wonderful project that combines the pleasures of fine food with the satisfaction of helping a truly worthy cause. On behalf of the MUHC and the Women's Health Mission, we thank you for purchasing this book and for supporting the health of women in our community, both right now and for generations to come.

Dr. Arthur T. Porter
Director General and CEO
The McGill University Health Centre

Dr. Seang-Lin Tan
Chief, Women's Health Mission
The McGill University Health Centre

# Contents

# Appetizers

Sesame Yellowfin Tuna with Baby Bok Choy, Yuzu and Sweet Soya Sauce

Pepper-Crusted Venison Carpaccio with a Basil-Chive Oil Shitake and Ginger

Spring Rolls with Sweet Mango Grilled Mediterranean Octopus Calamari

alla Luciana Whitefish Sashimi with Coriander Veal Carpaccio in White Wine

and a Salad of Grape Must and Crispy Parmesan Asparagus Vinaigrette

Figs Stuffed with Mahon Cheese and Serrano Ham Muffins à La Louisiane

Flatbread Lobster Carpaccio Seared Scallops, Fennel Purée and

Lemon Emulsion Braised Shitake Mushrooms with White Asparagus

Salmon Marinated in Yuzu Juice with Fresh Scallops and Caviar Astako

Dolmadakia Lobster-Stuffed Vine Leaves

# Sesame yellowfin tuna with baby bok choy, yuzu and sweet soya sauce

1 lb (450 g) tuna

Sea salt and freshly ground pepper

¼ cup (65 ml) white sesame seeds

¼ cup (65 ml) black sesame seeds

1 cup (250 ml) olive oil or grape seed oil

1 garlic clove, minced

1 tbsp (15 ml) minced pickled ginger

6 miniature bok choy, steamed until tender

Orange zest, fresh lemon balm or pickled ginger for garnish

Chili sauce (optional)


SAUCE:

¾ cup (190 ml) yuzu juice, or grapefruit juice

4 tbsp (60 ml) sweet soya sauce

4 tbsp (60 ml) mirin

4 tbsp (60 ml) grape seed oil

2 tbsp (30 ml) sesame oil

2 tbsp (30 ml) pickled ginger

1 tbsp (15 ml) Num Plum sauce (oyster sauce)

½ tsp (2 ml) Sambal Olek (chili paste)

To prepare sauce, whisk all sauce ingredients together in a medium-size bowl and set aside. Season tuna with salt and pepper. In a shallow bowl, combine black and white sesame seeds. Dredge tuna in the seeds, coating all surfaces (for a spicier dish, coat tuna with chili sauce prior to dredging in seeds).

Pour oil into medium-size frying pan (it should go about ¼ inch, or 6 mm, up the sides) and place over medium heat until hot. Sear tuna on all sides, approximately 1 minute per side (very little of the oil will be absorbed). Remove from pan and cover with foil to keep warm.

Remove almost all the oil from pan, then sauté garlic and pickled ginger for about 2 minutes over medium heat. Add baby bok choy and cook 2 minutes more. To serve, place bok choy at center of each plate. Cut tuna into ¼-inch (6 mm) slices and arrange over bok choy in a fan design. Drizzle with sauce and sprinkle with garnish. Remaining sauce can be used as a salad dressing or spooned over rice.

Serves 6

*Sesame Yellowfin Tuna with Bok Choy: Serving Size (336g), Calories 220, Total Fat 12g, Saturated Fat 2g, Cholesterol 30mg, Sodium 210mg, Total Carbohydrate 8g, Dietary Fiber 4g, Sugars 1g, Protein 23g*

*Sesame Yellowfin Tuna Sauce: Serving Size (30g), Calories 70, Total Fat 6g, Saturated Fat 0.5g, Cholesterol 0mg, Sodium 210mg, Total Carbohydrate 3g, Dietary Fiber 0g, Sugars 2g, Protein 0g*

SUGGESTED WINE PAIRING:

BERINGER
FOUNDERS' ESTATE

CABERNET SAUVIGNON
RED WINE · VIN ROUGE
CALIFORNIA

Cabernet Sauvignon Founder's Estate Beringer
Represented by: Maxxium

Yuzu juice

Venison

# Pepper-crusted venison carpaccio with a basil-chive oil

le Gourmand

12 oz (340 g) venison, from the leg

Freshly ground black pepper, enough to coat venison

1 tbsp (15 ml) plus ½ cup (125 ml) olive oil

½ cup (125 ml) fresh basil leaves

½ cup (125 ml) fresh chives

1 tsp (5 ml) Dijon mustard

2 small green onions, chopped

3½ oz (100 g) whole Parmesan, cut into slivers

Water for boiling

To prepare venison, add 1 tbsp (15 ml) oil to frying pan and heat to medium-high. While oil is heating, coat venison with pepper. Quickly sear meat on all sides, making sure to keep it very, very rare. Remove from pan, place on freezer-safe plate and put in freezer for 15-20 minutes (meat should be firm, but not frozen).

While venison is in freezer, bring water to boil and blanch basil and chives, about 10 seconds. Drain and place mixture in ice bath to retain bright green color. Drain again. Place basil and chives in a blender and blend with remaining olive oil and mustard until smooth. If mixture is too thick, add a bit of water. Remove meat from freezer and thinly slice. Divide over 4 plates, drizzle with basil-chive oil and garnish with green onions and Parmesan slivers.

Substitution: Beef tenderloin can be used instead of venison.

Serves 4

*Carpaccio: Serving Size (65g), Calories 115, Total Fat 6g, Saturated Fat 3g, Cholesterol 45mg, Sodium 230mg, Total Carbohydrate 1g, Dietary Fiber 0g, Sugars 1g, Protein 29g*

*Basil-Chive Oil: Serving Size (15g), Calories 90, Total Fat 10g, Saturated Fat 1.5g, Cholesterol 0mg, Sodium 10mg, Total Carbohydrate 0g, Dietary Fiber 0g, Sugars 0g, Protein 0g*

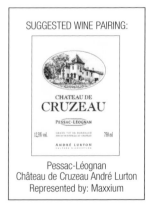

SUGGESTED WINE PAIRING:

CHATEAU DE CRUZEAU
PESSAC-LÉOGNAN
12.5% vol. 750 ml
ANDRÉ LURTON

Pessac-Léognan
Château de Cruzeau André Lurton
Represented by: Maxxium

# Shitake and ginger spring rolls with sweet mango

SPRING ROLLS:

1 tsp (5 ml) oil

4 oz (115 g) fresh shitake mushrooms, sliced

2 oz (60 g) carrots, julienned

2 oz (60 g) green zucchini, julienned

2 oz (60 g) bok choy, thinly sliced

1 oz (30 g) fresh ginger, julienned

Salt and white pepper

4 large-size rice papers

1 ripe, firm mango, cut into quarters

Black sesame seeds for garnish


SAUCE:

½ cup (125 ml) light soya sauce

1 tbsp (15 ml) oyster sauce

1 tbsp (15 ml) sesame oil

In heavy frying pan, heat oil on high until smoking. Sauté mushrooms 1 minute. Add carrots, zucchini, bok choy and ginger and toss together for 2 minutes. Put vegetable mixture in bowl and season with salt and pepper. Cool in refrigerator until ready to use (vegetables can be prepared a day in advance).

Soak rice papers one at a time in a bowl of warm water until softened. Remove from water and pat dry. Place one quarter of the vegetable mixture on each rice paper, top with one quarter of the mango and roll tightly, folding in sides so ends are closed.

To prepare sauce, whisk all 3 ingredients together. To serve spring rolls, cut in half so that one half is lying on plate, the other is standing. Drizzle sauce around rolls and garnish with sesame seeds.

Serves 4

*Spring Roll: Serving Size (181g), Calories 50, Total Fat 1.5g, Saturated Fat 0g, Cholesterol 0mg, Sodium 20mg, Total Carbohydrate 9g, Dietary Fiber 3g, Sugars 2g, Protein 2g*

*Sauce: Serving Size (30g), Calories 25, Total Fat 2.5g, Saturated Fat 0g, Cholesterol 0mg, Sodium 1360mg, Total Carbohydrate 0g, Dietary Fiber 0g, Sugars 0g, Protein 0g*

SUGGESTED WINE PAIRING:

Chardonnay Carneros Benziger
Family Winery
Represented by: Maxxium

Spring rolls

# Grilled Mediterranean octopus

estiatorio **Milos**

1 octopus tentacle, about 7 oz (200 g)

1 tbsp (15 ml) plus ½ tsp (2 ml) red wine vinegar

Pinch whole black peppercorns

Oregano to taste

2 tbsp (30 ml) cooked chickpeas

3 fresh bay leaves

Salt and white pepper

2 tbsp (30 ml) extra virgin olive oil

GARNISH:

Red and yellow Holland peppers, chopped

Vidalia onion, thinly sliced

Fresh dill and parsley, chopped

Capers

Heat oven to 500°F (260°C). Bake octopus in cooking tray with 1 tbsp (15 ml) red wine vinegar and peppercorns for 45 minutes, until partially cooked. Cool to room temperature.

While the octopus is cooking, using a small bowl, mix together the remaining vinegar, oregano, salt, pepper and most of the olive oil (the balance will be brushed onto the octopus).

Heat grill to high. Brush octopus with remaining oil. Cook on grill until hot inside, about 5 minutes, turning occasionally. Slice into ¼-inch (6 mm) rounds. Toss octopus and chickpeas with vinaigrette. Arrange on serving dish and garnish with peppers, onions, dill, parsley and capers.

Note: Octopus can be purchased at specialty fish markets. It should already have been properly tenderized.

Serves 2

*Serving Size (128g), Calories 220, Total Fat 15g, Saturated Fat 2g, Cholesterol 50mg, Sodium 230mg, Total Carbohydrate 4g, Dietary Fiber 0g, Sugars 0g, Protein 15g*

SUGGESTED WINE PAIRING:

Gerovassiliou White - Epanomi
50% Assyrtiko, 50% Malagousia
Imported by: Cava Spiliadis

# Calamari alla Luciana

1 cup (250 ml) Israeli couscous

¼ cup (65 ml) extra virgin olive oil

2 tbsp (30 ml) pine nuts

2 tbsp (30 ml) raisins

1 tbsp (15 ml) hot red pepper flakes

¼ cup (65 ml) caper berries

2 cups (500 ml) canned cherry tomatoes

1½ lbs (675 g) calamari tubes, cleaned
and cut into ¼-inch (6 mm) rounds

Kosher salt and freshly ground black pepper

3 green onions, sliced thinly

Prepare ice bath. Bring small pot filled with water to a boil and add salt. Add couscous and cook for 2 minutes. Drain and immediately plunge into ice bath. When couscous is cool, drain and set aside.

Using a heavy 12- or 14-inch (30-35 cm) frying pan, heat oil on medium-high until just smoking. Add pine nuts, raisins and red pepper flakes and sauté until pine nuts are golden-brown, about 2 minutes. Add caper berries, cherry tomatoes and couscous and bring to a boil. Add calamari, stir to mix and simmer for 2-3 minutes or until calamari is cooked (color should be opaque). Season with salt and pepper. To serve, ladle into 4 bowls and sprinkle with green onions.

Serves 4

*Serving Size (382g), Calories 510, Total Fat 19g, Saturated Fat 3g, Cholesterol 395mg, Sodium 410mg, Total Carbohydrate 49g, Dietary Fiber 4g, Sugars 7g, Protein 35g*

calamari

# Whitefish sashimi
## with coriander

12 oz (340 g) halibut, boneless and skinless

4 tsp (20 ml) sesame oil

Black sesame seeds and micro organic sprouts for garnish

SOYA AND MAPLE REDUCTION:

¼ cup (65 ml) maple syrup

¼ cup (65 ml) soya sauce

CORIANDER VINAIGRETTE:

3 tbsp (45 ml) chopped coriander

1 tbsp (15 ml) chopped chives

1 tbsp (15 ml) chopped shallots

3 tbsp (45 ml) olive oil

1 tbsp (15 ml) light soya sauce

½ tsp (2 ml) lemon zest

Juice of 1 lemon

In a small saucepan, prepare soya and maple reduction by heating liquids over medium heat until reduced to a syrupy consistency. Remove from heat. Prepare vinaigrette by mixing all the ingredients together.

Slice fish into ⅛-inch-thick (3 mm) filets and arrange on serving plate. In a heavy frying pan, heat sesame oil over high heat. Drizzle hot oil over fish to flash cook. Drizzle fish with vinaigrette and garnish with sesame seeds and sprouts. For the finishing touch, drizzle with soya-maple reduction.

Substitution: Mint or Thai basil can be used instead of coriander.

Serves 4

Sashimi: Serving Size (90g), Calories 130, Total Fat 6g, Saturated Fat 1g, Cholesterol 25mg, Sodium 45mg, Total Carbohydrate 0g, Dietary Fiber 0g, Sugars 0g, Protein 18g

Coriander Vinaigrette: Serving Size (46g), Calories 100, Total Fat 11g, Saturated Fat 1.5g, Cholesterol 0mg, Sodium 230mg, Total Carbohydrate 2g, Dietary Fiber 0g, Sugars 1g, Protein 1g

SUGGESTED WINE PAIRING:

Grande Cuvée Sparkling
Represented by: Whitehall Agencies

# Lamb carpaccio in white wine and a salad of grape must and crispy Parmesan

Restaurant
Yoyo

12 oz (340 g) finely sliced lamb loin

3½ oz (100 g) grated Parmesan

3 tbsp (45 ml) grape seed oil

2 tbsp (30 ml) aged vinegar, 20 or 40 years

2 shallots, finely minced

Salt and freshly ground black pepper

4 small bundles organic salad mix

12 grapes, peeled

1 tbsp (15 ml) grape must plus extra for garnish

Juice of ½ lemon

Heat oven to 350°F (180°C). Prepare Parmesan by placing cheese on non-stick baking sheet in 4 separate rounds. Cook for about 10 minutes. Let cool.

While Parmesan is crisping, in a small bowl mix together oil, vinegar, shallots, salt and pepper to make a vinaigrette. In a separate bowl, toss salad mix with grapes, 1 tbsp (15 ml) grape must and lemon juice. To serve, arrange lamb on plate and top with salad. Place cheese crisp on top, drizzle with vinaigrette and garnish with grape must.

Serves 4

*Serving Size (240g), Calories 360, Total Fat 24g, Saturated Fat 8g, Cholesterol 85mg, Sodium 560mg, Total Carbohydrate 8g, Dietary Fiber 3g, Sugars 5g, Protein 29g*

SUGGESTED WINE PAIRING:

Benjamin Brunel
Rasteau

Benjamin de Brunel - Rasteau
Represented by: Réserve et Sélection

Fresh
Parmesan

# Asparagus vinaigrette

24 large asparagus spears, ends trimmed

6 tbsp (90 ml) extra virgin olive oil

3 tbsp (45 ml) red wine vinegar

1 shallot, minced

Salt and freshly ground black pepper

3 tbsp (45 ml) grated Pecorino Romano

Bring water to a boil in a medium pot. Submerge asparagus for about 5 minutes, until tender but firm. Drain. In a small bowl, mix together oil, vinegar, shallots, salt and pepper. Lay asparagus on serving plate and drizzle with desired amount of vinaigrette. Sprinkle with cheese.

Serves 4

*Serving Size (149g), Calories 250, Total Fat 24g, Saturated Fat 4.5g, Cholesterol 10mg, Sodium 140mg, Total Carbohydrate 5g, Dietary Fiber 1g, Sugars 2g, Protein 6g*

# Figs stuffed with Mahon cheese and Serrano ham

4 fresh ripe figs

Olive oil for drizzling

Salt and freshly ground black pepper

2 oz (60 g) Mahon cheese

2 oz (60 g) Serrano ham, diced

1 oz (30 g) almonds, slivered and lightly toasted

Fruit syrup (optional)

Heat oven to 325°F (160°C). With the figs sitting plump side down with points facing skyward, use a sharp knife to make 2 perpendicular cuts across the top of the point and halfway down the fig, about ¼ inch (6 mm) deep. Drizzle figs with olive oil and sprinkle with salt and pepper. Place on cooking tray in oven and cook for 10 minutes.

While figs are cooking, mix together cheese and ham in a small bowl. Stuff figs with cheese-ham mixture. Place back in oven to broil. Remove when cheese is melted. Before serving, sprinkle with almond slivers and drizzle with fruit syrup, if desired.

Serves 4

*Serving Size (94g), Calories 160, Total Fat 9g, Saturated Fat 3.5g, Cholesterol 25mg, Sodium 85mg, Total Carbohydrate 13g, Dietary Fiber 3g, Sugars 11g, Protein 8g*

SUGGESTED WINE PAIRING:

HUNGARIA
*Grande Cuvée*
BRUT

Grande Cuvée Sparkling
Represented by: Whitehall Agencies

Fig

# Muffins à La Louisiane

*lalouisiane*

2½ cups (625 ml) flour

½ cup (125 ml) cornmeal

1½ tbsp (22 ml) baking powder

8½ tbsp (127 ml) butter

2 tbsp (30 ml) sugar

2 cups (500 ml) milk

¼ cup (65 ml) finely diced red pepper

¼ cup (65 ml) finely diced green pepper

½ jalapeno pepper, seeds removed and finely diced

½ tsp (2 ml) minced garlic

½ tbsp (8 ml) minced shallots

1 tsp (5 ml) La Louisiane spice mix *(see page 159)*

½ cup (125 ml) grated cheddar cheese (optional)

Heat oven to 350°F (180°C). In a large bowl, whisk together flour, cornmeal and baking powder. In a separate bowl, cream together butter and sugar. Beat in milk. Add remaining ingredients, mixing well. Add flour mixture until combined. Spoon batter into greased mini-muffin tins. Bake for 30-35 minutes.

Makes 48 muffins

*Serving Size (25g), Calories 60, Total Fat 3g, Saturated Fat 2g, Cholesterol 10mg, Sodium 80mg, Total Carbohydrate 7g, Dietary Fiber 0g, Sugars 1g, Protein 2g*

SUGGESTED WINE PAIRING:

VF

"Lasira"

RHÔNE VALLEY VINEYARDS

COSTIÈRES DE NÎMES
Appellation Costières de Nîmes Contrôlée

VIN ROUGE - RED WINE

Vin et Vaplein par La Vieille Ferme • Orange • France
PRODUIT DE FRANCE · PRODUCT OF FRANCE

250 ml      13 % alc./vol.

VF "Lasira" Costières-de-Nîmes
Represented by: Le Marchand de Vin

# Flatbread

TOWNE
HALL

4.4 lbs (2 kg) unbleached flour, or 1.5 kg flour plus .5 kg semolina flour

4 tsp (20 ml) salt

1 oz (30 g) fresh yeast, or 15 g dry yeast or 8 g instant yeast

5⅓ cups (1.33 l) water

⅓ cup (75 ml) olive oil plus extra for brushing

2 tsp (10 ml) sugar

Pinch each dried cumin, rosemary, thyme, oregano

Pinch toasted sesame seeds

Heat oven to 450°F (230°C). In the bowl of a standing mixer, whisk together flour and salt. In a separate bowl, pour yeast into water heated to 100°F (38°C). Add half of olive oil. Yeast is ready to use when foam appears, about 3-4 minutes. If no foam appears, discard mixture and begin again. Add yeast solution to flour mixture. Using the mixer's bread attachment, beat up to 30 minutes, until temperature increases by 3.1°F (1.5°C). Add remaining oil and beat for 1-2 minutes more. Remove dough from bowl and form into 24 balls. Brush each ball with olive oil and cover with plastic wrap and a dishtowel. Place in a dry area and let rise for about 30 minutes. Dough should double in size.

After dough has risen, uncover and knead twice (a pinch of flour on your hands will keep dough from sticking). Replace plastic wrap and dishtowels and let sit for 30 minutes more. To prepare dough for cooking, arrange in an oval shape (or any shape you wish). Using a sharp knife, score dough a few times from one end to the other. Brush with olive oil. Sprinkle with equal portions of cumin, rosemary, thyme, oregano and sesame seeds. Bake in oven for about 10 minutes.

Suggested toppings: salad with prosciutto and balsamic reduction, cheeses such as Parmesan, Fontana or buffalo mozzarella, apple and red pepper compote or cherry sun-dried tomatoes and black olives.

Note: Depending on the size of your standing mixer, you may have to halve or quarter the recipe.

Makes 24 loaves

*Serving Size (317g), Calories 1150, Total Fat 12g, Saturated Fat 1.5g, Cholesterol 0mg, Sodium 1160mg, Total Carbohydrate 219g, Dietary Fiber 9g, Sugars 3g, Protein 33g*

SUGGESTED WINE PAIRING:

Pinot Gris Bodega Lurton
Argentine JF Lurton
Represented by: Maxxium

# Orange-Pernod

# Lobster carpaccio

4 whole lobsters (recipe only uses tails)
1 head fennel cut into 12 slices
1 tsp (5 ml) mustard seed for garnish
Pinch fleur de sel

MIREPOIX:
1 carrot
1 stalk celery
1 leek, whites only
1 onion
2 sprigs each thyme, parsley and chives

ORANGE-PERNOD SAUCE:
4 cups (1l) orange juice without pulp
2 oz (60 ml) Pernod
2 tbsp (30 ml) sugar

To prepare sauce, bring orange juice, Pernod and sugar to a boil. Reduce liquid by three quarters. This should take 15-20 minutes. Let cool, then refrigerate. Sauce can be prepared a day in advance.

Thread a skewer lengthwise through each lobster to keep the tail straight. Bring large pot of water and *mirepoix* ingredients to a boil. Add lobsters and cook for 7-12 minutes, until tender. Place lobsters in cold water to cool. Remove skewers, then remove tails from lobsters. Use a sharp knife to cut between the meat and shell along one side of each tail. Remove the meat and slice thinly on the bias. Set aside.

Steam fennel for 2 minutes. Remove from heat. To serve, place 3 slices of steamed fennel on each plate and top with fanned-out lobster meat. Drizzle orange-Pernod sauce around plate, sprinkle with *fleur de sel* and garnish with mustard seed.

Serves 4

*Carpaccio: Serving Size (131g), Calories 90, Total Fat 0.5g, Saturated Fat 0g, Cholesterol 50mg, Sodium 310mg, Total Carbohydrate 5g, Dietary Fiber 2g, Sugars 0g, Protein 16g*

*Orange-Pernod Sauce: Serving Size (30g), Calories 20, Total Fat 0g, Saturated Fat 0g, Cholesterol 0mg, Sodium 0mg, Total Carbohydrate 4g, Dietary Fiber 0g, Sugars 4g, Protein 0g*

# Seared scallops, fennel purée and lemon emulsion

8 large, fresh U-10 scallops

Fleur de sel

2 tbsp (30 ml) grape seed or olive oil

Decorative herbs

## LEMON ZEST CONFIT:

1 cup (250 ml) lemon zest
(about 24 lemons are needed)

About ½ cup (125 ml) sugar

About ½ cup (125 ml) water

## LEMON CREAM:

1 cup (250 ml) lemon zest confit

1 cup (250 ml) 35% cream

1 cup (250 ml) milk

## FENNEL PURÉE:

1 fennel bulb, diced

¼ cup (65 ml) 35% cream

¼ cup (65 ml) milk

Salt and freshly ground black pepper

To make lemon zest confit, bring water to a boil and blanch 1 cup (250 ml) lemon zest. Drain. Blanch 2 more times, using fresh water each time. Place blanched and drained zest in a pot and cover with equal amounts sugar and water. Bring mixture to a boil. Remove from heat. Confit should have a syrupy consistency.

To make lemon cream, place lemon zest confit, cream and milk in a medium-size pot and simmer over low heat for 12-15 minutes. Using a blender, blend at high speed until texture becomes smooth. Prepare fennel purée by placing fennel in a medium-size pot with cream and milk. Cook over low heat until mixture is mushy. Season with salt and pepper to taste.

Heat heavy frying pan until very hot but not smoking. Pour in oil and wait a few seconds. Place scallops in pan and cook one side only until golden. Transfer scallops to paper towel. Brush with olive oil and sprinkle with *fleur de sel*. To serve, spoon fennel purée onto plate and top with decorative herbs and scallop. Drizzle with lemon cream.

Serves 4

*Scallops: Serving Size (133g), Calories 170, Total Fat 14g, Saturated Fat 5g, Cholesterol 35mg, Sodium 95mg, Total Carbohydrate 7g, Dietary Fiber 2g, Sugars 22g, Protein 7g*

*Lemon Cream: Serving Size (30g), Calories 50, Total Fat 4g, Saturated Fat 2.5g, Cholesterol 15mg, Sodium 10mg, Total Carbohydrate 3g, Dietary Fiber 0g, Sugars 3g, Protein 1g*

*Lemon Confit: Serving Size (30g), Calories 25, Total Fat 0g, Cholesterol 0mg, Sodium 0mg, Total Carbohydrate 7g, Dietary Fiber 0g, Sugars 5g, Protein 0g*

36

Seared scallops

# Braised shitake mushrooms
## with white asparagus

15 dried shitake mushrooms

16 oz (450 g) white asparagus, trimmed

2½ cups (625 ml) vegetable stock

16 oz (450 g) fresh mustard green hearts, center only

1 tsp (5 ml) vegetable oil

1 tsp (5 ml) salt

10 baby bok choy

1½ tsp (7 ml) sesame oil

1 tsp (5 ml) white wine

1 tsp (5 ml) soya sauce

1 green onion, chopped

1 medium-size piece ginger, minced

½ tsp (2 ml) sugar

1 tsp (5 ml) cornstarch

Soak mushrooms in warm water for several hours. Set aside until ready to use. Steam asparagus in ½ cup (125 ml) of the vegetable stock for 3 minutes. Drain and pat dry. Arrange asparagus along one side of a serving platter.

Cut mustard greens into 2-inch (5 cm) squares and blanch in boiling water for 10 seconds. Rinse in cold water and drain. In wok heated to medium-high, stir-fry greens in vegetable oil and 1 cup (250 ml) of the vegetable stock. Season with half the salt. Cook for 5 minutes. Drain and arrange on other side of serving platter.

Add baby bok choy to wok and stir-fry until tender. Remove and place in center of serving platter, draped over asparagus and greens. Remove mushrooms from water and add to wok with 1 cup (250 ml) of the vegetable stock, 1 tsp (5 ml) of the sesame oil, white wine, soya sauce, green onion, ginger and sugar. Steam for 20 minutes. Drain mushroom mixture, reserving liquid. Arrange mixture over bok choy in center of platter. Heat reserved liquid in a pot and season with remaining salt. Thicken by whisking in cornstarch. To serve, splash vegetables with remaining ½ tsp (2 ml) sesame oil and top with generous amount of mushroom stock.

Serves 4 to 6

*Serving Size (321g), Calories 90, Total Fat 2g, Saturated Fat 0g, Cholesterol 0mg, Sodium 600mg, Total Carbohydrate 15g, Dietary Fiber 5g, Sugars 3g, Protein 5g*

# Salmon marinated in yuzu juice with fresh scallops and caviar

4 fresh scallops in shells

7 oz (200 g) organic salmon, thinly sliced

2 shallots, minced

1 tbsp (15 ml) capers

4 tsp (20 ml) olive oil

4 tsp (20 ml) yuzu juice, or grapefruit juice

1⅓ oz (40 g) Corégone caviar

Young coriander sprouts (micro coriander)

Open scallops with a shucking knife, taking care not to damage the shells. Remove the scallop and reserve the juice for salmon mixture.

In a medium-size bowl, mix together the sliced salmon, shallots, capers, olive oil, yuzu juice and scallop juice. Stuff the 4 scallop shells with salmon mixture and top with a scallop. Garnish with a drop of caviar and a few coriander sprouts.

Serves 4

*Serving Size (96g), Calories 180, Total Fat 10g, Saturated Fat 1.5g, Cholesterol 95mg, Sodium 260mg, Total Carbohydrate 3g, Dietary Fiber 0g, Sugars 1g, Protein 18g*

SUGGESTED WINE PAIRING:

La Belle Terrasse
Chardonnay

Vin de Pays d'Oc,
Chardonnay La Belle Terrasse
Represented by: Maxxium

# Lobster

# Astako dolmadakia
## Lobster-stuffed vine leaves

t r i n i t y
*estiatorio*

2½ lbs (1.1 kg) whole gross lobster

**LOBSTER BROTH:**
1 carrot
3 celery stalks
1 onion
1 fennel bulb
2 garlic cloves
2 bay leaves
Pinch whole peppercorns

**AVGOLEMONO SAUCE:**
4 eggs at room temperature, separated
Juice of 3 lemons
2 cups (500 ml) reserved lobster broth
Salt and freshly ground black pepper

**STUFFING:**
1 onion, finely chopped
1 bunch green onions, chopped
1 bunch dill, chopped

1 bunch parsley, chopped
½ cup (125 ml) coarsely chopped dates
½ cup (125 ml) pine nuts
3 cups (750 ml) uncooked rice
Salt and freshly ground black pepper
½ cup (125 ml) olive oil
60 vine leaves

Bring 8 cups (2 l) cold water to a boil. Add lobster and cook for about 8 minutes. Place in cold water for 5 minutes to prevent further cooking. Remove meat from shells, keeping shells for broth. When meat is cool, finely chop and set aside. To prepare broth, place shells in large pot with all broth ingredients. Just cover with water, bring to a boil and simmer for 2½ hours with lid on. Strain through a fine sieve and set aside, reserving 2 cups (500 ml) for *avgolemono* sauce. While broth is cooking, make stuffing. In a large bowl, mix together all the ingredients except olive oil and vine leaves. Stir in chopped lobster. Refrigerate until ready to use. Just before broth is ready, boil vine leaves in water for 8-10 minutes, until soft but not soggy. Drain well.

To assemble vine leaves, flatten leaves one at a time, shiny side down. Place heaping tsp (5 ml) of stuffing in center of leaf. Fold edges over stuffing and roll tightly to form a compact cylinder. Repeat, using all the stuffing. In a large pot, place vine leaves closely together to prevent them from opening, up to 3 layers high. Cover with a plate to prevent them from floating. Add broth and olive oil, turn burner to low and cook, covered, for 30-45 minutes, or until rice has absorbed broth. Remove from pot and arrange on serving plate. Keep warm. To prepare *avgolemono* sauce, beat egg whites until they almost reach meringue stage. While still mixing, add egg yolks, lemon juice, reserved lobster broth, salt and pepper. Serve vine leaves topped with warm *avgolemono* sauce. Do not cover while still hot as eggs will cook.

Substitution: Minced beef, veal, lamb or chicken can be used instead of lobster.

Makes 60 rolls

*Serving Size (44g), Calories 80, Total Fat 3g, Saturated Fat 0g, Cholesterol 20mg, Sodium 40mg, Total Carbohydrate 11g, Dietary Fiber-less than 1g , Sugars 2g, Protein 3g*

# Salads

# Goat cheese medallions
## on a bed of mixed greens

**maestro** *S.V.P.*

**SAUCE:**

1 cup (250 ml) water

2 tsp (10 ml) cornstarch

2 cups (500 ml) port wine and raspberry sauce (sold in jar)

Salt and freshly ground black pepper

**SALAD:**

2 medallions goat cheese, 1 inch (2.5 cm) thick

1 tsp (5 ml) ground pistachios plus extra for garnish

1 tsp (5 ml) honey

4 handfuls mixed greens

Heat oven to 450°F (230°C). In a small bowl, whisk together water and cornstarch. In a medium-size pot on low burner, heat port wine and raspberry sauce until just warm. Whisk in salt and pepper. While whisking, add water-cornstarch mixture. Bring to a boil. Immediately remove from heat.

Place cheese medallions on baking sheet. Cover each medallion with half the pistachios. Spoon half the honey over the pistachios and place in oven. Remove from oven when cheese starts to melt, about 4 minutes. To serve, divide mixed greens between 2 plates and place cheese on top. Spoon sauce over top and sprinkle with pistachios.

Substitution: Port wine and raspberry sauce can be replaced with raspberry purée made from frozen raspberries processed in a food processor.

Serves 2

*Serving Size (87g), Calories 120, Total Fat 9g, Saturated Fat 6g, Cholesterol 20mg, Sodium 160mg, Total Carbohydrate 5g, Dietary Fiber 1g, Sugars 4g, Protein 7g*

SUGGESTED WINE PAIRING:

MARLBOROUGH
Sauvignon Blanc
Oyster Bay
NEW ZEALAND

Sauvignon Blanc Marlborough
Oyster Bay Winery
Represented by: Maxxium

# Seared scallops with fennel, orange and spinach salad

½ cup (125 ml) plus 2 tbsp (30 ml) extra virgin olive oil

12 large scallops

Salt and freshly ground black pepper

2 tbsp (30 ml) fresh orange juice

2 tbsp (30 ml) fresh lemon juice

1 large fennel bulb, thinly sliced

6 oz (170 g) fresh spinach

1 orange, peeled and cut into sections

Cherry tomatoes, halved, for garnish

Heat 2 tbsp (30 ml) of the olive oil in a large, heavy, non-stick frying pan until hot but not smoking. Season scallops generously with salt and pepper. Add scallops to pan and sauté both sides until golden-brown and opaque in the middle, about 3 minutes. Transfer to plate and cover with foil.

To prepare vinaigrette, whisk remaining olive oil with orange juice and lemon juice. Add salt and pepper to taste. Combine fennel, spinach and orange sections in a large bowl. Toss with three quarters of the vinaigrette. Divide salad among 4 plates. Put 3 scallops on each plate and drizzle with remaining vinaigrette. Garnish with cherry tomatoes.

Serves 4

*Serving Size (222g), Calories 410, Total Fat 34g, Saturated Fat 4.5g, Cholesterol 30mg,*
*Sodium 230mg, Total Carbohydrate 15g, Dietary Fiber 5g, Sugars 4g, Protein 13g*

SUGGESTED WINE PAIRING:

Cuvèe Brut Prosecco d.o.c.
Carpené Malvolti
Offered by: Italvine

# Roasted beet, walnut and goat cheese salad

**Taverne SUR LE SQUARE**

1 lb (450 g) assorted beets
such as red, yellow and striped

Mixed greens such as baby spinach,
arugula and field mix

1 cup (250 ml) walnut halves, roasted
*(see note)*

1 cup (250 ml) unripened goat cheese
such as Tournevent

## VINAIGRETTE:

½ cup (125 ml) chopped shallots

1½ cups (375 ml) port wine

2 tsp (10 ml) sugar

½ cup (125 ml) red wine vinegar

1 tsp (5 ml) salt

1¼ cups (315 ml) olive oil

Heat oven to 400°F (200°C). Wrap beets in aluminum foil, shiny side facing in, and place in shallow baking tray. Roast for 40-90 minutes or until easily pierced with a knife. Remove from oven and let cool slightly. Wearing rubber gloves, rub beets to remove skins. When cool enough to handle, slice into quarters.

While beets are roasting, prepare vinaigrette. Place shallots in a small pot and add port wine to cover. Heat over medium-high, stirring constantly. Be careful not to burn. When port has almost evaporated, remove from heat and allow to cool. Purée mixture in blender with sugar, vinegar and salt. Slowly add olive oil until emulsified. To serve, toss beets and greens together and place in a serving bowl. Drizzle with 1-2 tbsp (15-30 ml) of the vinaigrette and top with roasted walnuts and goat cheese.

Note: In oven heated to 400°F (200°C), roast walnut halves for 5-10 minutes, being careful not to burn. The leftover vinaigrette can be reserved for later use.

Serves 4

*Salad: Serving Size (223g), Calories 370, Total Fat 25g, Saturated Fat 7g, Cholesterol 20mg, Sodium 250mg, Total Carbohydrate 18g, Dietary Fiber 6g, Sugars 9g, Protein 12g*

*Vinaigrette: Serving Size (30g), Calories 100, Total Fat 9g, Saturated Fat 1g, Cholesterol 0mg, Sodium 80mg, Total Carbohydrate 2g, Dietary Fiber 0g, Sugars 2g, Protein 0g*

SUGGESTED WINE PAIRING:

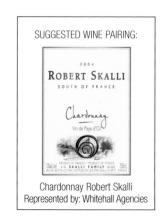

Chardonnay Robert Skalli
Represented by: Whitehall Agencies

# Spinach salad
## with marinated shrimp

Pintx
cuisine espagnole

14 oz (400 g) Matane shrimp, cooked

½ red pepper, finely chopped

½ green pepper, finely chopped

½ yellow pepper, finely chopped

⅓ Spanish onion, finely chopped

1 avocado, cubed

2 tsp (10 ml) black sesame seeds

¼ cup (65 ml) sesame oil

2 tsp (10 ml) balsamic vinegar

Juice of 2 lemons

Salt and freshly ground black pepper

4 small bunches spinach

In a large bowl, mix together first 10 ingredients until evenly combined. Season with salt and pepper to taste. Arrange spinach on 4 plates and top with shrimp salad.

Serves 4

*Serving Size (281g), Calories 350, Total Fat 23g, Saturated Fat 3.5g, Cholesterol 195mg, Sodium 320mg, Total Carbohydrate 14g, Dietary Fiber 6g, Sugars 3g, Protein 24g*

SUGGESTED WINE PAIRING:

Bonterra
VINEYARDS
CHARDONNAY
MENDOCINO COUNTY
ORGANICALLY GROWN GRAPES

Bonterra Chardonnay
Represented by: Charton Hobbs

53

# Traditional Greek salad

estiatorio **Milos**

2 vine-ripened tomatoes, chopped into chunks

1 green pepper, sliced into strips

¼ cucumber, sliced crosswise

½ Vidalia onion, thinly sliced

1 tsp (5 ml) dried oregano

1 tsp (5 ml) sea salt

½ tsp (2 ml) freshly ground black pepper

3 tbsp (45 ml) extra virgin olive oil

1 tsp (5 ml) red wine vinegar

6 kalamata olives

2 slices feta cheese

Fresh basil leaves and small marinated spicy peppers for garnish

Combine tomatoes, green peppers, cucumbers and onions in a bowl with oregano, salt and black pepper. Add olive oil and vinegar and toss well. Arrange salad on plate and top with olives, feta and garnishes.

Serves 2

*Serving Size (312g), Calories 380, Total Fat 33g, Saturated Fat 9g, Cholesterol 35mg, Sodium 1770mg, Total Carbohydrate 16g, Dietary Fiber 4g, Sugars 8g, Protein 8g*

SUGGESTED WINE PAIRING:

**OVILOS**
REGIONAL WHITE WINE OF PANGEON
VIN BLANC DE PAYS DE PANGÉE
2006
PRODUCT OF GREECE / PRODUIT DE GRÈCE
750 ml - 13% alc./vol.

Ovilos Regional White - Kavala
50% Assyrtiko, 50% Semillon
Imported by: Cava Spiliadis

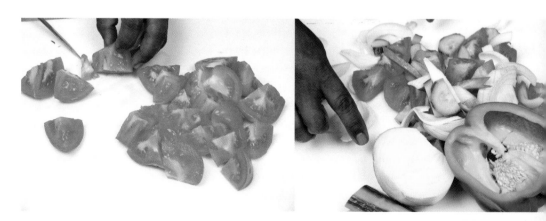

# Radicchio, endive, pecan and orange salad

¼ cup (65 ml) pecans, roasted

½ head radicchio, sliced

1 endive, sliced crosswise

1 sweet orange, peeled and sectioned

2 tbsp (30 ml) olive oil

1 tbsp (15 ml) balsamic vinegar

Salt and freshly ground black pepper

Chives for garnish

Heat oven to 300°F (150°C). On a baking sheet, roast pecans for 5-7 minutes. Let cool. Toss remaining ingredients together in a bowl. Add pecans and toss again. Serve garnished with chives.

Serves 4

*Serving Size (186g), Calories 150, Total Fat 12g, Saturated Fat 1.5g, Cholesterol 0mg, Sodium 30mg, Total Carbohydrate 10g, Dietary Fiber 6g, Sugars 4g, Protein 3g*

SUGGESTED WINE PAIRING:

Grand Ardèche
CHARDONNAY
Louis Latour

Chardonnay Grand Ardèche
Louis Latour
Represented by: Maxxium

# Insalata Orientale

1 lb (450 g) mixed lettuce

3 tbsp (45 ml) soya sauce

3 tbsp (45 ml) honey

2 tbsp (30 ml) red wine vinegar

½ cup (125 ml) peanut butter

½ tsp (2 ml) red chili flakes

½ tsp (2 ml) salt

½ tsp (2 ml) freshly ground black pepper

4 tbsp (60 ml) vegetable oil

Julienned carrots and tempura crumbs for garnish

Rinse and dry lettuce. Cut into 2-inch (5 cm) pieces.

To prepare vinaigrette, whisk together all remaining ingredients except vegetable oil. While whisking, slowly add oil until the ingredients are well blended. Toss with lettuce and garnish with carrots and tempura crumbs.

Serves 4

*Serving Size (196g), Calories 390, Total Fat 30g, Saturated Fat 4g, Cholesterol 0mg, Sodium 870mg, Total Carbohydrate 25g, Dietary Fiber 5g, Sugars 16g, Protein 11g*

SUGGESTED WINE PAIRING:

Sogrape Reserva Douro White
Represented by: Charton Hobbs

Chili
flakes

# Rock shrimp

# Crunchy endives, rock shrimp salad, ginger and mandarins in a blood orange vinaigrette

**cuisine inspirée**

4 endives, julienned

1 English cucumber, peeled and very thinly sliced lengthwise

2 blood oranges, peeled and cut into sections

Chives, finely chopped

8 oz (225 g) rock shrimp, peeled and deveined

4 small mandarins, peeled and quartered

VINAIGRETTE:

Juice of 4 blood oranges

3 tbsp (45 ml) ginger, peeled and chopped

1 tsp (5 ml) rice vinegar

Pinch each salt and white pepper

½ cup (125 ml) plus 1 tbsp (15 ml) olive oil

Before making the vinaigrette, reserve 2 tbsp (30 ml) blood orange juice. Place remaining juice, ginger, rice vinegar, salt and pepper in a blender. With blender running, slowly add ½ cup (125 ml) of the olive oil in a stream until liquid is emulsified. If vinaigrette is too spicy, add more olive oil.

In a large bowl, toss together endives, cucumber, blood orange sections and chives. Toss again with desired amount of vinaigrette. Arrange salad on serving plate.

In a heavy frying pan heated to high, sauté shrimp in remaining 1 tbsp (15 ml) olive oil until golden and tender. Deglaze with reserved blood orange juice. Remove from heat. Arrange beside salad on serving plate. Place mandarins around shrimp.

Substitution: Regular oranges and a handful of raspberries can be used instead of blood oranges.

Serves 4

*Serving Size (973g), Calories 600, Total Fat 36g, Saturated Fat 5g, Cholesterol 85mg, Sodium 200mg, Total Carbohydrate 54g, Dietary Fiber 23g, Sugars 27g, Protein 20g*

SUGGESTED WINE PAIRING:

CHAMPAGNE
Charles Heidsieck
REIMS
BRUT RÉSERVE

Champagne Brut Réserve
Charles Heidsieck
Represented by: Maxxium

# Slow-roasted red and yellow beet and shrimp salad

## BEETS:

3 baby red beets, whole

3 yellow beets, whole

Grape seed oil for brushing beets

2 tsp (10 ml) sugar cane, or brown sugar

## VINAIGRETTE:

¼ cup (65 ml) grape seed oil

3 tbsp (45 ml) white balsamic vinegar

1 tbsp (15 ml) lemon-infused balsamic vinegar, or Vino Cotto with fig vinegar

Reserved beet juice

Sea salt and freshly ground black pepper

## SHRIMP:

6 jumbo black tiger shrimps, peeled and deveined

1½ cups (375 ml) baby arugula

1 avocado, diced or sliced

8 berry capers

8 jumbo kalamata olives

Red and yellow cherry tomatoes, about 6 each

Sliced red onion for garnish

Adjust oven rack to middle position and heat oven to 350°F (180°C). Brush red and yellow beets with oil, sprinkle with sugar cane and wrap in foil. Place on a cooking tray and slow roast for about 40 minutes, or until beets are tender. Remove from oven, reserving the juices. While beets are still warm, remove skin (it should peel off easily). When cool enough to handle, cut each beet into 6 wedges.

Heat grill to medium-high. While grill is heating, make vinaigrette by whisking together the oil, both vinegars and the reserved beet juice. Season with salt and pepper. Pour 2 tbsp (30 ml) of the vinaigrette into a separate bowl and use to coat shrimps. Grill shrimps for about 2 minutes per side, rotating continually to avoid charring. Overcooking will dry shrimps out.

In a bowl, mix together beets, arugula, avocado, capers, olives, tomatoes and grilled shrimp. Drizzle with desired amount of vinaigrette, leaving some aside to add at the last minute, and toss well. Season to taste with salt and pepper. Garnish with red onion slices and drizzle with leftover vinaigrette.

Note: Use kitchen gloves to avoid staining your hands while removing the skin from the beets.

Serves 3

*Serving Size (246g), Calories 290, Total Fat 22g, Saturated Fat 3g, Cholesterol 15 mg, Sodium 370mg, Total Carbohydrate 21g, Dietary Fiber 8g, Sugars 10g, Protein 6g*

SUGGESTED WINE PAIRING:

Les Vignes Retrouvées Blanc
Represented by: Whitehall Agencies

# Crab and lobster salad

1¼ lbs (570 g) lobster, cooked

1 cup (250 ml) Dungeness crab, cooked

1 cup (250 ml) blue crab, cooked

1 cup (250 ml) snow crab, cooked

1 tbsp (15 ml) mayonnaise

1 tbsp (15 ml) white port wine

1 tbsp (15 ml) chopped capers

1 tbsp (15 ml) finely chopped shallots

1 tsp (5 ml) Dijon mustard

Juice of ½ lemon

Piri-piri or Tabasco sauce to taste

Pinch chopped chives

Crouton toast for garnish

PARSLEY OIL:

⅓ cup (85 ml) chopped parsley

⅔ cup (170 ml) extra virgin olive oil

Chop seafood into small pieces. Place in a large bowl, add remaining ingredients and mix well. Season with parsley oil, which is made by mixing together the ingredients and refrigerating (parsley oil will keep for several months, and the longer it sits, the more concentrated the flavor will become). Accompany salad with crouton toast.

Note: If one or more of these crab types is unavailable, a single type can be used, or even canned crab.

Serves 4 to 6

*Serving Size (224g), Calories 270, Total Fat 8g, Saturated Fat 1g, Cholesterol 180mg, Sodium 820mg, Total Carbohydrate 3g, Dietary Fiber 0g, Sugars 1g, Protein 43g*

SUGGESTED WINE PAIRING:

PRODUIT DE FRANCE
VIN BLANC — Vin d'Alsace — PRODUCT OF FRANCE
WHITE WINE
APPELLATION ALSACE CONTROLEE

Pfaffenheim

GEWURZTRAMINER

Pfaffenheim Gewurztraminer
Represented by: Charton Hobbs

# Pomegranate and beet juice salad with apple and red pepper compote

TOWNE HALL

**SALAD:**

1 large beet

4 small bunches baby mesclun salad

4 small bunches baby arugula

6 oz (170 g) hard goat cheese

Extra virgin olive oil

Edible flowers for garnish

**POMEGRANATE SYRUP:**

1 cup (250 ml) fresh or frozen pomegranate seeds, about 2 pomegranates

1 cup (250 ml) pomegranate juice

½ cup (125 ml) sugar

**APPLE AND RED PEPPER COMPOTE:**

2 tbsp (30 ml) butter

4-5 Granny Smith apples, peeled and diced

1 red pepper, diced

¼ cup (65 ml) white port wine

¼ cup (65 ml) sugar

1 tsp (5 ml) salt

1 tsp (5 ml) cayenne pepper

**BEET JUICE:**

3 beets

1 cup (250 ml) water

Sprig each rosemary and thyme

Salt

Heat oven to 350°F (180°C). To prepare salad, wrap the large beet in foil and bake for 45-60 minutes, until tender. When cool enough to handle, peel and slice very thin. In the meantime, make pomegranate syrup by cooking all the ingredients in a pot over low heat, uncovered, until reduced by two thirds. Strain. It should have a honey-like consistency.

To make compote, melt butter in a heavy frying pan over high heat. Sear apples and peppers for about 3 minutes. Add remaining ingredients and simmer for about 3 minutes, until sugar dissolves. Apples and peppers should still be crunchy. Cool by setting pan in tray of ice water. To prepare beet juice, put water in a pot and boil beets until tender. Add rosemary and thyme 5 minutes before beets are done cooking. Reserve water. Discard rosemary and thyme. When cool enough to handle, peel beets, then purée in blender. Pass through a French sieve twice. Combine beet purée and reserved water in a pot, season with salt and boil until reduced to syrup. Pass syrup through a sieve or cheesecloth.

To serve, arrange sliced beets on a serving plate so they overlap. Spoon compote onto beets and top with mesclun, arugula and goat cheese. Drizzle with pomegranate reduction, beet reduction and oil. Garnish with edible flowers.

Serves 4

*Compote: Serving Size (401g), Calories 480, Total Fat 6g, Saturated Fat 3.5g, Cholesterol 15mg, Sodium 690mg, Total Carbohydrate 107g, Dietary Fiber 5g, Sugars 94g, Protein 2g*

*Salad: Serving Size (113g), Calories 170, Total Fat 13g, Saturated Fat 9g, Cholesterol 35mg, Sodium 290mg, Total Carbohydrate 5g, Dietary Fiber 1g, Sugars 3g, Protein 10g*

SUGGESTED WINE PAIRING:

VISION

Cono Sur

PINOT NOIR

Pinot Noir Vision Cono Sur
Represented by: Maxxium

# Roasted cherry tomato salad

4 vines cherry tomatoes, about 6 tomatoes per vine

2 Spanish onions, sliced 1 inch (2.5 cm) thick

2 tbsp (30 ml) olive oil

Salt and freshly ground black pepper

½ cup (125 ml) feta, crumbled

1 tsp (5 ml) dried oregano

Sprig of fresh oregano

Heat oven to 450°F (230°C). With tomatoes still on vine, brush with olive oil and season with salt and pepper. Repeat with onion slices. Keeping separate, roast onions and tomatoes with vines in oven. Remove tomatoes after 8 minutes. Roast onions for 2-4 minutes more. Let cool. To serve, arrange onion slices on serving plate and top with tomatoes. Garnish with crumbled feta, dried oregano and oregano sprig. Drizzle with olive oil.

Serves 4

*Serving Size (183g), Calories 150, Total Fat 11g, Saturated Fat 4g, Cholesterol 15mg, Sodium 220mg, Total Carbohydrate 10g, Dietary Fiber 2g, Sugars 4g, Protein 4g*

# Caprese salad with buffalo mozzarella and vine tomatoes

2 slices olive bread

2 tbsp (30 ml) extra virgin olive oil

1 8-oz (225 g) ball buffalo mozzarella, cut into 6 slices

1 vine tomato, cut into slices

Salt and freshly ground black pepper

8 red and yellow cherry tomatoes, quartered

1 green onion, finely sliced

10 oregano leaves, chopped

6 basil leaves, chopped

2 slices prosciutto, each sliced into 4 strips

Balsamic glaze for garnish

Chive oil for garnish (optional)

Heat oven to 350°F (180°C). Cut bread into cubes. In a bowl, toss bread cubes with 1 tbsp (15 ml) of the olive oil. Place bread cubes on cookie sheet and bake for 5-10 minutes, until crisp. Set aside.

Arrange the mozzarella and tomato slices around the center of a serving plate. Drizzle with olive oil and season with salt and pepper. Top with cherry tomatoes, green onion, oregano, basil and prosciutto. Add warm croutons and drizzle with balsamic glaze. Garnish with chive oil, if desired.

Serves 3

*Serving Size (169g), Calories 220, Total Fat 9g, Saturated Fat 1.5g, Cholesterol 20mg, Sodium 720mg, Total Carbohydrate 11g, Dietary Fiber 3g, Sugars 2g, Protein 24g*

SUGGESTED WINE PAIRING:

campogrande
ORVIETO
CLASSICO

ANTINORI

Orvieto Classico
Campogrande Antinori
Represented by: Maxxium

Caprese

# Soups

# Noodles in seafood soup

3 cups (750 ml) fish stock, homemade if possible

2 tsp (10 ml) fish bouillon

2 tsp (10 ml) hoisin sauce

4 oz (115 g) vermicelli noodles, soaked in water according to package instructions

10 mussels in shells

4 clams in shells

2 shrimps, peeled and deveined

Over high heat, bring fish stock, bouillon and hoisin sauce to a boil. Add vermicelli, mussels and clams and cook until mussels and clams open, about 4 minutes (discard any that don't open). Add shrimps and cook another 2 minutes. Ladle into bowls and serve.

Note: If scallops (already shelled) are being included in the soup, add to pot at the same time as shrimps.

Serves 2

*Serving Size (533g), Calories 230, Total Fat 5g, Saturated Fat 1g, Cholesterol 45mg, Sodium 910mg, Total Carbohydrate 20g, Dietary Fiber-less than 1g, Sugars 2g, Protein 23g*

Hot&sour

# Hot and sour beef rice noodle soup

3 dried shitake mushrooms

¼ cup (65 ml) sliced bamboo shoots

1 6-oz (170 g) filet mignon, sliced crosswise

10 baby bok choy

¼ cup (65 ml) vegetable oil

2 tsp (10 ml) Szechuan hot chili and bean paste

2 tsp (10 ml) chopped green onions

2 tsp (10 ml) light soya sauce

6 cups (1.5 l) chicken stock

1 tsp (5 ml) salt

6 oz (170 g) broad sticky rice noodles, cooked

2 tsp (10 ml) Chinese rice vinegar

1 tsp (5 ml) sesame oil

1 tsp (5 ml) freshly ground black pepper

Hot peppers for garnish

Soak mushrooms and bamboo shoots in warm water for several hours. Drain and cut into thin strips. Steam strips until done. Cut baby bok choy in half lengthwise and steam for 3 minutes. Set these ingredients aside.

Heat vegetable oil in wok on high. Stir in hot chili and bean paste and green onions. Add soya sauce and chicken stock and bring to a boil. Let boil for about 2 minutes. Season with salt. Add filet slices, mushrooms, bamboo shoots and baby bok choy. Add rice noodles and bring to a boil once again. Reduce heat and season with splash of rice vinegar and sesame oil. Serve with a sprinkle of pepper and hot peppers for garnish.

Substitution: Tofu or chicken can be used instead of beef.

Serves 2 to 6

*Serving Size (345g), Calories 220, Total Fat 17g, Saturated Fat 4.5g, Cholesterol 20mg, Sodium 1230mg, Total Carbohydrate 10g, Dietary Fiber-less than 1g, Sugars 1g, Protein 7g*

SUGGESTED WINE PAIRING:

Madiran Château Peyros
Represented by: Maxxium

# Carrot, celery root and leek soup

1 tbsp (15 ml) unsalted butter

½ cup (125 ml) thinly sliced onion

1 cup (250 ml) thinly sliced leeks

1 tsp (5 ml) grated fresh ginger

Fleur de sel

2 cups (500 ml) peeled, thinly sliced carrots

2 cups (500 ml) peeled, coarsely chopped celery root

1 cup (250 ml) chopped parsley

Pinch fresh thyme

4½ cups (1.1l) chicken stock

4 tbsp (60 ml) low-fat sour cream

8 pecans, toasted and chopped

Freshly ground black pepper

Melt butter in a large pot over medium-high heat. Add onions and leeks and sauté until soft. Add ginger and salt and cook for 2 minutes more. Add carrots, celery root, parsley, thyme and stock and bring to a boil. Reduce heat, cover pot and allow soup to simmer until vegetables are tender, about 30-40 minutes.

Remove pot from heat and blend mixture in batches in blender. Return to pot and simmer for 2 minutes. Season with salt and pepper. Serve in warm bowls garnished with sour cream and toasted pecans.

Note: If soup is too thick, thin with a touch of water.

Serves 4

*Serving Size (483g), Calories 160, Total Fat 7g, Saturated Fat 3g, Cholesterol 15mg, Sodium 900mg, Total Carbohydrate 23g, Dietary Fiber 5g, Sugars 9g, Protein 4g*

celery root

# Glace de chou-fleur au caviar

**cuisine inspirée**

1 cauliflower, cut into bite-size pieces

2 tbsp (30 ml) olive oil

4 oz (115 g) shallots, minced

2 cups (500 ml) chicken stock

½ tsp (2 ml) salt

½ tsp (2 ml) freshly ground black pepper

¼ cup (65 ml) Beluga caviar

2 sprigs mixed herbs for garnish

In a large, heavy frying pan, heat olive oil over high heat and sauté shallots until softened. Add chicken stock and season with salt and pepper. Continue cooking until mixture begins to boil. Add cauliflower. Reduce heat to low and continue cooking for 15-20 minutes. The cauliflower must be well done and very soft. Remove pan from heat.

Working in batches, purée mixture in blender. Season again, if necessary. Pour mixture into a freezer-safe container and place in freezer for about 2 hours. Remove from freezer and blend again to break up any lumps. Mixture should have the consistency of a smoothie. Serve chilled with a dollop of caviar and garnish of fresh herbs.

Serves 4

*Serving Size (317g), Calories 150, Total Fat 10g, Saturated Fat 1.5g, Cholesterol 75mg, Sodium 890mg, Total Carbohydrate 13g, Dietary Fiber 4g, Sugars 5g, Protein 7g*

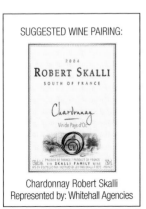

SUGGESTED WINE PAIRING:

2004
ROBERT SKALLI
SOUTH OF FRANCE

Chardonnay
Vin de Pays d'Oc

Chardonnay Robert Skalli
Represented by: Whitehall Agencies

# American lobster bisque
## with fennel confit
## and pan-seared bay scallops

4 giant bay scallops

1 tsp (5 ml) butter

Salt and freshly ground pepper

Caviar for garnish


FENNEL CONFIT:

8 oz (225 g) fennel, sliced

1 tsp (5 ml) olive oil

Salt to taste

Pinch sugar


BISQUE:

1 tbsp (15 ml) butter

2 shallots, thinly sliced

2 button mushrooms, thinly sliced

1 cup (250 ml) brandy

1 cup (250 ml) Madeira wine

6 cups (1.5 l) lobster stock


BEURRE-MANIE

1 tbsp (15 ml) butter, softened

2 tbsp (30 ml) flour

To prepare fennel confit, place fennel in a pot with olive oil, salt and sugar. Cover and cook on low heat for about 20 minutes. Set aside until ready to use.

To prepare bisque, melt butter in a stockpot over medium-high heat. Sauté shallots until golden-brown, about 3 minutes. Add mushrooms and cook until slightly browned, about 2 more minutes. Remove from heat. Add ¾ cup (190 ml) of the brandy and ¾ cup (190 ml) of the Madeira wine (remaining brandy and wine will be used later for seasoning). Return shallot mixture to high heat and allow liquid to reduce by half. Add lobster stock and bring to a boil. Reduce heat to simmer and cook uncovered for 15-20 minutes (weaker stocks may need to cook longer to achieve concentrated flavors). Occasionally skim and discard foam that may rise to top while bisque is simmering.

To prepare *beurre-manie,* mix butter and flour with fingers to form a smooth paste. Press paste onto end of a whisk. When bisque achieves a strong, almost salty flavor, whisk in *beurre-manie* until dissolved. Cook 5 more minutes over high heat, whisking occasionally. Strain through fine sieve, making sure to extract all juices. Season with reserved brandy and wine and keep warm.

Season scallops with salt and pepper. In a non-stick pan over medium-high heat, melt butter and sear scallops on both sides until golden-brown. To serve, ladle bisque into shallow bowl, place fennel confit in center and top with sliced scallop and dollop of caviar. Serve immediately.

Serves 4

*Serving Size (512g), Calories 380, Total Fat 9g, Saturated Fat 4.5g, Cholesterol 25mg, Sodium 640mg, Total Carbohydrate 11g, Dietary Fiber 0g, Sugars 7g, Protein 12g*

SUGGESTED WINE PAIRING:

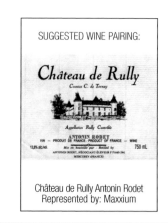

Château de Rully Antonin Rodet
Represented by: Maxxium

Bisque

# Mushroom, soya and coriander consommé

GLOBE

8 cups (2 l) vegetable stock, homemade if possible

2 cups (500 ml) shitake mushrooms

1 cup (250 ml) edamame, fresh or frozen

1 tbsp (15 ml) low-sodium soya sauce

Salt and freshly ground black pepper

½ cup (125 ml) chopped coriander

Heat stock in pot over medium-high until reduced by one quarter. Add mushrooms and continue to reduce until 4 cups (1 l) of stock remain. Add edamame and cook until tender. Season with soya sauce, salt and pepper. Top with chopped coriander.

Serves 4

*Serving Size (590g), Calories 120, Total Fat 3g, Saturated Fat 0g, Cholesterol 0mg, Sodium 810mg, Total Carbohydrate 18g, Dietary Fiber 4g, Sugars 1g, Protein 6g*

SUGGESTED WINE PAIRING:

Viognier Domaine des Salices
JF Lurton
Represented by: Maxxium

# Roasted butternut squash soup with julienned Granny Smith apples and white truffle oil

8 oz (225 g) butternut squash, cut into chunks

2 oz (60 g) leeks, white parts only, diced

3 oz (85 g) carrots, diced

1 oz (30 g) onions, diced

1 tbsp (15 ml) butter

4 cups (1 l) chicken stock

Pinch grated nutmeg

Pinch cinnamon

Salt and freshly ground black pepper

1 Granny Smith apple, unpeeled and julienned

White truffle oil

In a medium-size pot, sauté squash, leeks, carrots and onions in butter. Add stock and, using a wooden spoon, deglaze vegetables. Add nutmeg and cinnamon and let simmer until vegetables are tender, about 20 minutes.

In a food processor or blender, working in batches, blend soup to a fine pulp. Season with salt and pepper. Ladle soup into bowls. Place julienned apples in center and drizzle with truffle oil.

Serves 4

*Serving Size (374g), Calories 90, Total Fat 3.5g, Saturated Fat 2g, Cholesterol 10mg, Sodium 730mg, Total Carbohydrate 16g, Dietary Fiber 3g, Sugars 8g, Protein 2g*

SUGGESTED WINE PAIRING:

Les Vignes Retrouvées Blanc
Represented by: Whitehall Agencies

Butternut

# Pasta & Rice

# Tagliatelle with wild mushrooms

2 tbsp (30 ml) olive oil

½ medium onion, diced

2 large garlic cloves, flattened

12 oz (340 g) mixed fresh mushrooms such as oyster, portobello and crimini, stems removed

4 oz (115 g) fresh or frozen porcini mushrooms

¼ cup (65 ml) dry white wine

½ cup (125 ml) chicken broth

Salt and freshly ground black pepper

1 lb (450 g) tagliatelle noodles

2 tbsp (30 ml) unsalted butter

1 bunch arugula

Truffle oil for drizzling

2 tbsp (30 ml) chopped basil

2 tbsp (30 ml) chopped parsley

½ cup (125 ml) grated Parmigiano-Reggiano

Heat oil in a large, heavy frying pan over medium-high heat. Sauté onion and garlic until slightly browned. Add mushrooms and continue to sauté until caramelized. Slowly add white wine, scraping the bottom of pan with a wooden spoon to deglaze. Add chicken broth and cook on medium until mixture slightly thickens. Add salt and pepper to taste.

Cook pasta in large pot of boiling water according to package instructions. Remove from heat when pasta is tender but still firm. Drain well and add to mushroom sauce in pan, keeping heat on medium. Toss with butter.

Transfer pasta to a large bowl and top with arugula. Drizzle with truffle oil and garnish with basil, parsley and Parmigiano-Reggiano.

Serves 4

*Serving Size (542g), Calories 850, Total Fat 22g, Saturated Fat 10g, Cholesterol 40mg, Sodium 680mg, Total Carbohydrate 110g, Dietary Fiber 12g, Sugars 8g, Protein 46g*

# Risotto ai funghi porcini e tartufo bianco

Ristorante
## Primo & Secondo

3 cups (750 ml) porcini bouillon,
or chicken or vegetable stock

5 tbsp (75 ml) butter at room temperature

½ onion, finely chopped

4 oz (115 g) fresh porcini mushrooms, diced

4 oz (115 g) risotto rice

2 oz (60 g) dried porcini mushrooms,
soaked in water, then diced

½ oz (15 g) Parmesan, grated

1 tsp (5 ml) white truffle oil

Sprigs of thyme for garnish

In a saucepan, bring bouillon to a boil. Set aside. Using a deep frying pan, melt 3 tbsp (45 ml) of the butter at medium heat. Sauté onion for 2 minutes, stirring often so the onion doesn't darken. Stir in porcini mushrooms. Add risotto rice and stir for 2-3 minutes. Mix in dried porcini mushrooms.

Pour ladleful of hot bouillon into onion mixture and stir slowly until liquid is absorbed. Repeat this step until risotto is tender and creamy, about 25 minutes. Remove risotto from heat and add remaining butter, Parmesan cheese and truffle oil. Stir well to combine. Garnish each serving with thyme sprig.

Serves 2 as a main dish, 4 as a side dish

*Serving Size (285g), Calories 320, Total Fat 18g, Saturated Fat 10g, Cholesterol 40mg, Sodium 420mg, Total Carbohydrate 32g, Dietary Fiber 3g, Sugars 2g, Protein 10g*

*Habs Captain, Saku Koivu*
*"Whenever I'm at Primo & Secondo I order this risotto. The mushrooms and truffles are perfect together."*

SUGGESTED WINE PAIRING:

BARBI

BRUNELLO
DI MONTALCINO
FATTORIA
dei BARBI

Brunello di Montalcino
Fattoria dei Barbi
Represented by: Maxxium

92

# Pear and gorgonzola risotto

2 pears, peeled and cored

2 tbsp (30 ml) butter

1 small onion, chopped

2 tbsp (30 ml) vegetable oil

1 cup (250 ml) risotto rice

5 oz (150 ml) dry white wine

4 cups (1 l) vegetable stock

2 oz (60 g) Gorgonzola

2 oz (60 g) Parmesan, grated

Salt and freshly ground black pepper

Chives, chopped, for garnish

Cut a few thin pear slices for garnish and cube the rest. Place 1 tsp (5 ml) of the butter in a frying pan, heat to medium and lightly brown cubes. Set aside. Add pear slices to same pan and gently brown. Set aside.

In a casserole on medium heat, sauté onion in vegetable oil until brown. Turn heat to low, stir in rice and cook for 1 minute, making sure the rice absorbs any liquid in pan. Add wine and allow to evaporate. Add enough vegetable stock to cover rice, then stir until stock is absorbed. Repeat this step until all stock is absorbed and rice is creamy. About 20 minutes before serving, add cubed pears and Gorgonzola. Stir until cheese is melted. Remove from heat and stir in remaining butter and Parmesan. Season with salt and pepper to taste. Serve garnished with pear slices and chopped chives.

Serves 4

*Serving Size (498g), Calories 510, Total Fat 22g, Saturated Fat 9g, Cholesterol 35mg, Sodium 170mg, Total Carbohydrate 58g, Dietary Fiber 4g, Sugars 15g, Protein 14g*

SUGGESTED WINE PAIRING:

BAROLO

2003

FONTANAFREDDA

Fontanafredda Barolo D.O.C.G.
Represented by: Whitehall Agencies

# Jambalaya

*la louisiane*

1 tbsp (15 ml) oil

½ cup (125 ml) diced smoked ham

½ cup (125 ml) diced uncooked sausage

½ cup (125 ml) diced uncooked chicken

1 cup (250 ml) chopped celery

½ cup (125 ml) chopped red onion

½ cup (125 ml) chopped red pepper

½ cup (125 ml) chopped green pepper

1 tsp (5 ml) minced garlic

3 cups (750 ml) long grain rice, uncooked

1½ cups (375 ml) canned tomatoes

2 tbsp (30 ml) La Louisiane spice mix *(see page 159)*

6 cups (1.5 l) fish, veal or chicken stock

4 oz (115 g) shrimps, peeled and deveined

Heat oven to 400°F (200°C). In a large, deep, ovenproof frying pan, heat oil to medium-high and sauté ham, sausage and chicken until browned. Scrape bottom of pan to keep meat from sticking.

Add celery, onion, red and green peppers and garlic and sauté until tender but still firm. Keep scraping bottom of pan to avoid sticking. Stir in rice, tomatoes and spice mix. Pour in stock and reduce heat to medium. Cover pan with foil and place in oven for 30-40 minutes, until most of the liquid has been absorbed and rice is tender. Stir in shrimps in last 5 minutes and cover until done.

Serves 6 to 8

*Serving Size (395g), Calories 400, Total Fat 9g, Saturated Fat 2.5g, Cholesterol 50mg, Sodium 780mg, Total Carbohydrate 62g, Dietary Fiber 2g, Sugars 4g, Protein 18g*

spices smoked ham

SUGGESTED WINE PAIRING:

CLOS DU BOIS.

CABERNET SAUVIGNON
*Sonoma County*

Cabernet Sauvignon
Sonoma County Clos du Bois
Represented by: Maxxium

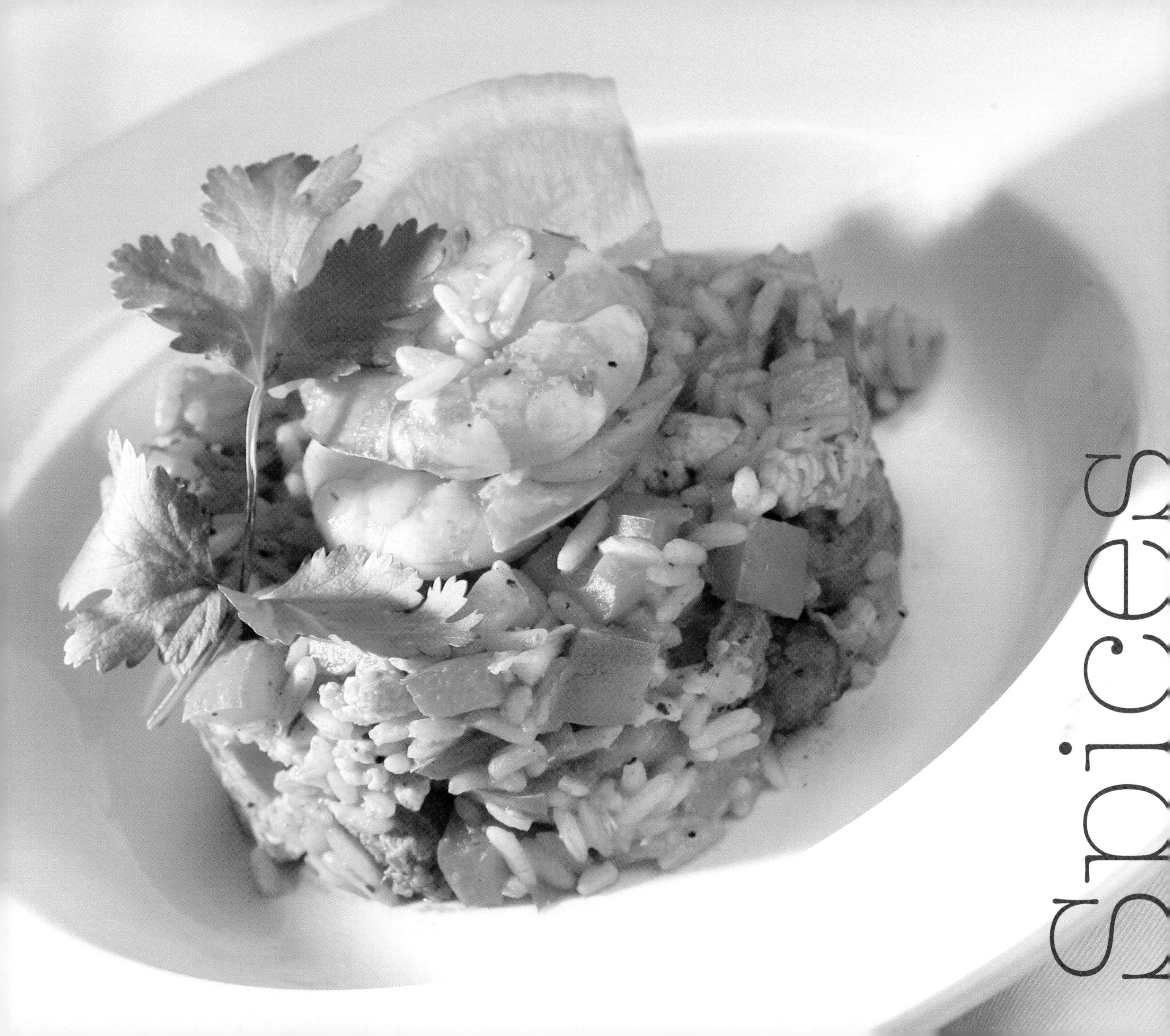

# Spices

# Lobster pasta

3 oz (85 g) fresh lobster

1 tbsp (15 ml) olive oil

2 tbsp (30 ml) chopped fresh Roma tomatoes

2 tbsp (30 ml) chopped wild mushrooms

1 tbsp (15 ml) slivered garlic

Pinch red pepper flakes

¼ cup (65 ml) white wine

½ cup (125 ml) chicken stock

½ cup (125 ml) tomato sauce

¾ cup (190 ml) lobster bisque

7 oz (200 g) fresh Chitarucci pasta

2 tbsp (30 ml) butter

1 tbsp (15 ml) grated Parmesan

2 tbsp (30 ml) chopped basil

1 tbsp (15 ml) chopped parsley

Bring a pot of water to a boil. Add lobster and cook for 3 minutes. Immediately place in bowl of cold water to prevent further cooking (it will be partially cooked at this point). Cut into chunks.

Heat olive oil in heavy frying pan over high heat. When oil begins to smoke, add tomatoes and mushrooms. Cook about 30 seconds or until lightly browned. Add garlic and red pepper flakes and cook 45 seconds more. Deglaze skillet with white wine and allow liquid to reduce a bit. Add chicken stock, tomato sauce and lobster bisque. Keeping skillet at high heat, reduce liquid by three quarters. This should take about 5 minutes.

Drop pasta into boiling water. As soon as it floats (this should take less than 1 minute), drain and mix into sauce, which is still on high heat. Add butter and Parmesan and stir until butter and cheese melt. Add lobster chunks, basil and parsley and cook for another minute. Garnish with a drizzle of olive oil before serving.

Serves 1

*Serving Size (879g), Calories 820, Total Fat 42g, Saturated Fat 18g, Cholesterol 195mg, Sodium 2030mg, Total Carbohydrate 66g, Dietary Fiber 6g, Sugars 8g, Protein 37g*

SUGGESTED WINE PAIRING:

Pacific Rim - White
Represented by: Réserve et Sélection

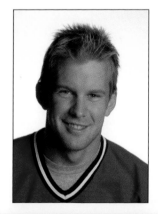

*Habs defenseman Mike Komisarek highly recommends Bice's Lobster Pasta, his favorite meal in town!*

# Whole wheat spaghetti with fava beans, pizelli and cherry tomatoes

**Vino Rosso**
RISTORANTE • CUISINE ITALIENNE

14 oz (400 g) whole wheat spaghetti

4 tbsp (60 ml) olive oil

2 garlic cloves, minced

½ cup (125 ml) fava beans, fresh or frozen

½ cup (125 ml) green peas, fresh or frozen

½ cup (125 ml) cherry tomatoes

Salt and freshly ground black pepper

Parmesan (optional)

Whole basil leaves for garnish

Bring a small pot of water to a boil and add pasta. Cook until tender but firm. Drain. While pasta is cooking, heat olive oil and garlic in a frying pan at medium heat until golden. Add fava beans, peas, cherry tomatoes, salt and pepper and stir well to incorporate. With heat still at medium, stir in cooked pasta. Serve topped with Parmesan and a garnish of basil.

Serves 4

*Serving Size (180g), Calories 510, Total Fat 15g, Saturated Fat 2g, Cholesterol 0mg, Sodium 45mg, Total Carbohydrate 82g, Dietary Fiber 15g, Sugars 5g, Protein 17g*

SUGGESTED WINE PAIRING:

Chianti Castiglioni d.o.c.g.
Marchesi de' Frescobaldi
Offered by: Italvine

# A simple pasta sauce

4 tbsp (60 ml) vegetable oil

¾ cup (190 ml) chopped onion

½ lb (225 g) ground veal

1  28-oz (840 g) can Italian plum tomatoes, drained and diced

Salt and freshly ground black pepper

2 cups (500 ml) fresh spaghetti or other noodle

½ cup (125 ml) grated Parmigiano-Reggiano cheese

Fresh basil for garnish

Heat oil in a frying pan over high heat. Add onions and sauté for a few seconds. Add veal and sauté until cooked. Lower heat to medium-low, add tomatoes and simmer for 10-12 minutes. Season with salt and pepper to taste.

While sauce is simmering, cook pasta according to package instructions. Drain. Serve sauce over pasta and top with cheese. Garnish with basil.

Serves 4

*Serving Size (414g), Calories 450, Total Fat 22g, Saturated Fat 4.5g, Cholesterol 55mg, Sodium 360mg, Total Carbohydrate 42g, Dietary Fiber 4g, Sugars 9g, Protein 22g*

SUGGESTED WINE PAIRING:

INSOGLIO
del cinghiale

Campo di Sasso
· Bibbona ·

TOSCANA

IGT Toscana, Insoglio del Cinghiale,
Tenuta di Biserno
Represented by: Maxxium

# Penne del giorno

Restaurant **Prima Luna**

3 cups (750 ml) thin string beans, cut into bite-size pieces

1 1-lb (450 g) package penne

20 cherry tomatoes, quartered

2-3 oz (30-45 ml) olive oil

4-6 basil leaves, torn up

3 garlic cloves, sliced thin (optional)

Whole basil leaves for garnish

Bring a large pot of salted water to a boil. Add beans and cook for about 8 minutes. Remove from water. While water is still boiling, add penne. Cook for about 7 minutes. Add cooked beans and boil for 1 minute more.

Drain pasta and beans and place in a bowl. Add tomatoes, drizzle with olive oil and top with basil and garlic. Toss well. Garnish with basil leaves and serve.

Serves 4

*Serving Size (310g), Calories 620, Total Fat 16g, Saturated Fat 2.5g, Cholesterol 0mg, Sodium 1180mg, Total Carbohydrate 102g, Dietary Fiber 8g, Sugars 7g, Protein 19g*

# String beans

# Market vegetable linguini

12 oz (340 g) linguini

1 tsp (5 ml) olive oil

1 cup (250 ml) julienned zucchini

1 cup (250 ml) chopped onion

1 cup (250 ml) green onion, cut diagonally

1 cup (250 ml) julienned red and yellow peppers

1 cup (250 ml) julienned carrots

10 sun-dried tomatoes, julienned

Salt and freshly ground black pepper

PESTO:

2 cups (500 ml) fresh basil

1 cup (250 ml) olive oil

¼ cup (65 ml) grated Parmesan

2 garlic cloves

Salt and freshly ground black pepper

---

Prepare pesto by combining all ingredients in a blender or food processor. Bring 8 cups (2 l) water to a boil. Add a pinch of salt. Drop in pasta and cook to desired tenderness.

While pasta is cooking, add olive oil to a heavy frying pan heated to high and sauté vegetables for 3-4 minutes. Do not overcook. Drain pasta and pour into a bowl. Add pesto and vegetables and mix together.

Serves 4

*Serving Size (371g), Calories 830, Total Fat 59g, Saturated Fat 9g, Cholesterol 65mg, Sodium 160mg, Total Carbohydrate 63g, Dietary Fiber 9g, Sugars 9g, Protein 16g*

SUGGESTED WINE PAIRING:

**Fortant Merlot**
Represented by: Whitehall Agencies

# Fish

# Halibut on a bed of lentils

2 8-oz (225 g) pieces halibut

Salt and freshly ground black pepper

1 tbsp (15 ml) clarified butter


LENTIL MIXTURE:

1 shallot, chopped

¼ cup (65 ml) red wine

¾ cup (190 ml) demi-glace, bottled

2 star anise buds

1 cinnamon stick

Salt and freshly ground black pepper

1 cup (250 ml) precooked lentils

2 prosciutto slices, chopped

¼ cup (65 ml) 35% cream (optional)

Prosciutto slices and roasted red pepper strips for garnish

Heat oven to 350°F (180°C). Season fish with salt and pepper to taste. Melt butter in frying pan over medium heat. Sear fish on both sides and continue cooking until a hint of color appears. Remove from pan and place in an ovenproof dish. Cook in oven for 4-6 minutes, until fish is flaky.

Using the same pan, sauté shallots. With a wooden spoon, deglaze pan while adding red wine. Stir in demi-glace, star anise, cinnamon stick, salt and pepper. Bring to a boil. Immediately remove from heat and strain. Discard star anise and cinnamon stick. Return strained mixture to pan and add lentils and chopped prosciutto. Stir in cream, if desired. Serve fish over lentil mixture and garnish with prosciutto and roasted peppers.

Suggested side dish: blanched asparagus and carrots.

Serves 2

*Halibut: Serving Size (234g), Calories 300, Total Fat 11g, Saturated Fat 4.5g, Cholesterol 90mg, Sodium 180mg, Total Carbohydrate 0g, Dietary Fiber 0g, Sugars 0g, Protein 47g*

*Lentil Mixture: Serving Size (205g), Calories 370, Total Fat 9g, Saturated Fat 3g, Cholesterol 15mg, Sodium 2680mg, Total Carbohydrate 43g, Dietary Fiber 4g, Sugars 4g, Protein 19g*

SUGGESTED WINE PAIRING:

*Chardonnay*
APPELLATION BOURGOGNE CONTRÔLÉE

*Louis Latour*
MIS EN BOUTEILLE PAR LOUIS LATOUR NÉGOCIANT-ÉLEVEUR
A BEAUNE - CÔTE-D'OR - FRANCE

Bourgogne Chardonnay
Louis Latour
Represented by: Maxxium

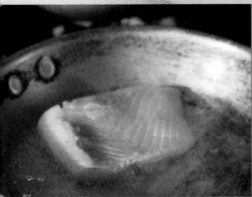

Halibut & lentils

# Seared tuna with lemon-anchovy vinaigrette

6 oz (170 g) French green beans

½ tsp (2 ml) whole coriander seeds

½ tsp (2 ml) whole black peppercorns

½ tsp (2 ml) fennel

½ tsp (2 ml) sea salt

2  8-oz (225 g) pieces #1 Yellowfin tuna

1 tbsp (15 ml) olive oil


GARNISH:

2 ripe plum tomatoes

2 cups (500 ml) olive oil


VINAIGRETTE:

2 tbsp (30 ml) red wine vinegar

2 tbsp (30 ml) lemon juice

1 tbsp (15 ml) capers

1 shallot, minced

1-2 anchovy filets

½ cup (125 ml) olive oil

¼ tsp (1 ml) salt


To prepare garnish, cut tomatoes in half lengthwise and remove pulp and seeds. Place in a small pot and add enough oil to submerge completely. Poach over low heat for a half hour. Remove from oil and allow to cool. In the meantime, bring a medium-size pot of salted water to a boil. Add green beans and boil for a couple of minutes, until cooked but still firm. Drain and cool.

To prepare vinaigrette, purée red wine vinegar, lemon juice, capers, shallot and anchovy filets in blender. Slowly add olive oil while blending to make an emulsion. Add salt to taste.

To prepare tuna, combine coriander seeds, peppercorns and fennel in a spice grinder and grind coarsely. Put spice mixture in a small bowl and stir in sea salt. Roll tuna in spice mixture until well coated. Heat oil in a heavy frying pan over high heat until almost smoking. Sear tuna for 30 seconds on all sides. Remove from pan and set aside. Toss green beans with 1-2 tbsp (15-30 ml) of the vinaigrette and arrange over 4 plates. Slice tuna into ⅛-inch-thick (5 mm) slices and lay over green beans. Top with poached tomato halves and sprinkle with salt.

Note: The olive oil left over from poaching the tomatoes can be reserved for later use in pastas and sauces, as can the vinaigrette, which makes enough to serve 10-14 people.

Serves 4

SUGGESTED WINE PAIRING:

GREG NORMAN ESTATES

*Limestone Coast*
**Cabernet Merlot**

Cabernet Merlot Greg Norman Estates
Represented by: Maxxium

*Tuna: Serving Size (115g), Calories 120, Total Fat 1g, Saturated Fat 0g, Cholesterol 50mg, Sodium 330mg, Total Carbohydrate 0g, Dietary Fiber 0g, Sugars 0g, Protein 27g*

*Garnish: Serving Size (69g), Calories 20, Total Fat 0g, Saturated Fat 0g, Cholesterol 0mg, Sodium 5mg, Total Carbohydrate 3g, Dietary Fiber 1g, Sugars 2g, Protein 1g*

*Vinaigrette: Serving Size (19g), Calories 70, Total Fat 8g, Saturated Fat 1g, Cholesterol 0mg, Sodium 310mg, Total Carbohydrate 1g, Dietary Fiber 0g, Sugars 0g, Protein 0g*

*Chantal Chamandy*
*"The seared tuna from the Taverne makes a perfect light dinner or summer lunch."*

# Szechuan-style steamed whole sea bass with piment rouge soya bean and chili sauce

1 whole sea bass, cleaned and scaled, about 2 lbs (900 g)

2 tsp (10 ml) Szechuan-fermented soya beans

1 tsp (5 ml) finely chopped hot red pepper, seeded

1 tsp (5 ml) chopped ginger

1 tsp (5 ml) rice wine

1 tsp (5 ml) light soya sauce

1 tsp (5 ml) salt

1 tsp (5 ml) shredded ham (optional)

1 tsp (5 ml) chopped green onion

2 tsp (10 ml) vegetable oil, heated

Fried onions (optional)

Rinse soya beans. In a bowl, toss together soya beans, hot red peppers, ginger, rice wine, soya sauce, salt and ham (if using). Place fish on large platter (spine facing up), and sprinkle with soya bean mixture. Place platter with fish in a boiling steamer over high heat for about 10 minutes or until fish is thoroughly cooked. Remove from steamer, sprinkle with green onion and drizzle with hot vegetable oil. Garnish with fried onions, if desired.

Note: After fish has been scaled and cleaned, it should be split lengthwise from gills down without cutting through the back. The back bone should be cut in sections, rubbed with ½ tsp (2 ml) salt and left to sit for 5 minutes before cooking.

Serves 4

*Serving Size (235g), Calories 240, Total Fat 7g, Saturated Fat 1.5g, Cholesterol 95mg, Sodium 820mg, Total Carbohydrate 0g, Dietary Fiber 0g, Sugars 0g, Protein 42g*

Sea Bass

salmon

# Salmon in a red wine sauce with prosciutto and braised lentils

## SALMON:

4 6-oz (170 g) organic or wild salmon filets, without skin

2 tbsp (30 ml) olive oil

4 thin slices good quality prosciutto for garnish

## WINE REDUCTION:

1 tbsp (15 ml) olive oil

3 tbsp (45 ml) finely chopped shallots

Cracked black pepper to taste

Juice of ½ lemon

3 cups (750 ml) red wine

2 tbsp (30 ml) unsalted butter

## LENTILS:

1 cup (250 ml) dry lentils

1 tbsp (15 ml) olive oil

1 tbsp (15 ml) finely chopped shallots

¾ cup (190 ml) carrots, diced

¾ cup (190 ml) green beans in ½-inch (12 mm) pieces

Pinch fresh thyme, chopped

Sea salt and white pepper

To prepare wine reduction, heat oil in frying pan over medium-high heat. Add shallots and pepper and sauté for a few minutes. Add lemon juice and wine and allow to simmer until sauce has been reduced to a little more than ½ cup (125 ml). Remove from heat. Add butter just before serving.

While reduction is simmering, cook lentils in boiling water with a pinch of sea salt until tender. Drain lentils, reserving ½ cup (125 ml) of the cooking water.

In a second frying pan, heat oil over medium-high heat. Add shallots, carrots and green beans. Sauté for a few minutes, then stir in thyme, lentils and reserved cooking water. Season with salt and pepper. Keep warm.

Heat a non-stick frying pan with 2 tbsp (30 ml) olive oil to medium-high. Cook salmon filets on both sides until medium-rare. Serve over warm lentils drizzled with wine reduction. Garnish each plate with slice of prosciutto.

Serves 4

SUGGESTED WINE PAIRING:

ANTONIN RODET
DEPUIS 1875

BOURGOGNE A. RODET
APPELLATION BOURGOGNE CONTRÔLÉE
PINOT NOIR

MIS EN BOUTEILLE PAR - BOTTLED BY ANTONIN RODET AT F 71640-294 - FRANCE
VIN - PRODUIT DE FRANCE          PRODUCT OF FRANCE - WINE

Bourgogne Pinot Noir
Antonin Rodet
Represented by: Maxxium

*Salmon & Prosciutto: Serving Size (201g), Calories 280, Total Fat 13g, Saturated Fat 2g, Cholesterol 105mg, Sodium 320mg, Total Carbohydrate 0g, Dietary Fiber 0g, Sugars 0g, Protein 38g*

*Wine Reduction: Serving Size (195g), Calories 210, Total Fat 9g, Saturated Fat 4g, Cholesterol 15mg, Sodium 10mg, Total Carbohydrate 4g, Dietary Fiber 0g, Sugars 0g, Protein 1g*

*Lentils: Serving Size (189g), Calories 210, Total Fat 4g, Saturated Fat 0.5g, Cholesterol 0mg, Sodium 340mg, Total Carbohydrate 32g, Dietary Fiber 12g, Sugars 5g, Protein 13g*

# Pan-seared Chilean sea bass
## with roasted red pepper salad

2 sweet red peppers, whole

2 tsp (10 ml) extra virgin olive oil

2 garlic cloves, minced

1 tsp (5 ml) chopped Italian parsley

Salt and freshly ground black pepper

4  6-oz (170 g) pieces fresh Chilean sea bass

Green parsley oil (optional)

Balsamic vinegar (optional)

Heat grill or broiler to high. Grill or broil peppers until evenly roasted. Remove from heat, place in bowl and cover with plastic wrap. When peppers have cooled, remove skin with the help of a dry towel. Rinse under cool water to remove excess skin, then drain. Slice peppers into long strips. Add to a medium-size bowl along with 1 tsp (5 ml) oil, garlic and parsley. Toss until mixed. Season with salt and pepper.

Heat remaining 1 tsp oil in heavy frying pan on medium-high. Rinse sea bass under cold water and pat dry. Season with salt and pepper. Sear in pan on both sides, about 3 minutes per side. Arrange pepper mixture over 4 plates and top with cooked fish. Drizzle with green parsley oil and balsamic vinegar, if desired.

Serves 4

*Serving Size (163g), Calories 150, Total Fat 4g, Saturated Fat 1g, Cholesterol 55mg, Sodium 90mg, Total Carbohydrate 4g, Dietary Fiber 1g, Sugars 2g, Protein 25g*

SUGGESTED WINE PAIRING:
### Cakebread Cellars

NAPA VALLEY
**Sauvignon Blanc**
Sauvignon Blanc Napa Valley
Cakebread Cellars
Represented by: Maxxium

# Grilled salmon with pasta

*estiatorio* **Milos**

6 8-oz (225 g) salmon filets

Salt and white pepper

MARINADE:

1 cup (250 ml) extra virgin olive oil

⅓ cup (85 ml) freshly squeezed lemon juice

PASTA:

½ cup (125 ml) olive oil

8 garlic cloves, crushed

2 fresh hot red peppers, seeded
and finely chopped

Large bunch basil, chopped and divided

Pinch salt

1 lb (450 g) fettuccini

Capers and hot red pepper,
thinly sliced, for garnish

To prepare marinade, whisk together extra virgin olive oil and lemon juice. Divide liquid into 2 bowls (half will be used to marinate the filets, the other half as a sauce once the salmon is cooked). Season filets with salt and pepper. Dip each filet into marinade and coat on all sides. Discard marinade.

To prepare dressing for pasta, in a small saucepan, add oil, garlic, hot red peppers and handful of basil. Heat on medium until garlic fragrance is released. Do not overcook. Remove from heat and stir in salt.

Drop pasta into large pot of rapidly boiling salted water and cook until done but still firm. Drain and transfer to serving bowl. Pour dressing over pasta and garnish with handful of basil and slivers of red pepper.

While pasta is cooking, heat grill to medium. Grill filets, starting with flesh side, for about 8 minutes, turning fish to achieve grill marks on all sides. Remove from grill and dip hot filets into marinade in second bowl and coat on all sides. Serve with pasta.

Serves 6

*Salmon: Serving Size (231g), Calories 360, Total Fat 19g, Saturated Fat 3g, Cholesterol 125mg, Sodium 100mg, Total Carbohydrate 0g, Dietary Fiber 0g, Sugars 0g, Protein 45g*

*Pasta: Serving Size (127g), Calories 460, Total Fat 20g, Saturated Fat 3g, Cholesterol 0mg, Sodium 10mg, Total Carbohydrate 60g, Dietary Fiber 3g, Sugars 3g, Protein 11g*

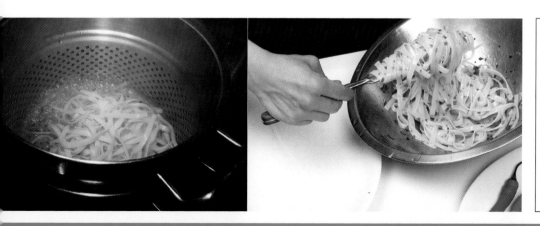

SUGGESTED WINE PAIRING:

Domaine Katsaros Red - Krania
85% Cabernet Sauvignon, 15% Merlot
Imported by: Cava Spiliadis

# Spiced tuna

1 tbsp (15 ml) fresh lemon juice

1 tbsp (15 ml) tamari sauce

1 tbsp (15 ml) balsamic vinegar

¼ cup (65 ml) olive oil

1 tbsp (15 ml) coriander seeds

1 tsp (5 ml) dill seeds

1 tsp (5 ml) anise seeds

1 tsp (5 ml) fennel seeds

Pinch caraway tea

1 grain of cardamom

4 6-oz (170 g) pieces tuna

2 tbsp (30 ml) vegetable oil

Salt

In a small bowl, whisk together lemon juice, tamari sauce and balsamic vinegar. While whisking, slowly pour in olive oil to make an emulsion. Grind all spices together and place on a plate. Gently dredge tuna in spices to coat one side only.

Heat vegetable oil in heavy frying pan over high heat until hot but not smoking. Sear tuna on spice side first, then on other side. Remove and lightly season with salt. Place seared tuna in a bowl and pour in lemon juice mixture. Serve with a cannellini salad, tomato salad, lentil salad or grilled potato slices.

Serves 4

*Serving Size (205g), Calories 380, Total Fat 23g, Saturated Fat 2.5g, Cholesterol 75mg, Sodium 320mg*
*Total Carbohydrate 3g, Dietary Fiber-less than 1g, Sugars 1g, Protein 41g*

SUGGESTED WINE PAIRING:

IGT Rosso del Veronese
BROLO DI CAMPOFIORIN
Represented by: Maxxium

Tuna

# Grilled Portuguese cod

4 pieces salted cod

1 red or yellow pepper, halved

2 tbsp (30 ml) olive oil plus extra for brushing

12 small new potatoes, boiled and halved

1 Spanish onion, sliced long and thin

1 garlic clove, minced

Chili sauce to taste

Salt and freshly ground black pepper

2 tbsp (30 ml) red wine vinegar

2 tbsp (30 ml) chopped parsley

16 black olives

1 bunch rapini, or baby broccoli

4 slices prosciutto for garnish (optional)

Heat grill to high. Brush cod with olive oil on flesh side. Sear, flesh side down. Continue cooking on grill for 10 more minutes. Cook in oven heated to 350°F (180°C) for 15 minutes.

While cod is cooking, brush pepper pieces with olive oil and grill until soft. Slice into thin strips. Grill or pan-fry potatoes until lightly browned. Set peppers and potatoes aside. In a frying pan over high heat, sauté onion in 2 tbsp (10 ml) of the olive oil until lightly browned. Add garlic and chili sauce and season with salt and pepper. Reduce heat to medium. Add red wine vinegar, parsley and black olives and cook 2 minutes more. Just before serving, add potatoes and pepper strips to pan and heat through.

In the meantime, boil rapini in salt water until tender. Drain. Serve fish over rapini and top with onion mixture. Garnish with prosciutto, if desired.

Note: Salted cod must be soaked in cold water for 24 to 48 hours before using, and the water must be changed 2 or 3 times.

Serves 4

Serving Size (636g), Calories 480, Total Fat 19g, Saturated Fat 2.5g, Cholesterol 100mg, Sodium 830mg, Total Carbohydrate 30g, Dietary Fiber 4g, Sugars 4g, Protein 46g

SUGGESTED WINE PAIRING:

curva
DOURO

Douro Curva White
Sogevinus Wine
Represented by: Maxxium

# Grilled salmon, black pepper emulsion, black olive-sweet pickle-caper salsa served with endive salad

**primadonna**
RISTORANTE & BAR SUSHI

### FISH AND EMULSION:

4 6-oz (170 g) pieces salmon

4 tbsp (60 ml) black peppercorns, soaked in water overnight

4 tbsp (60 ml) pine nuts, roasted (see note)

1 cup (250 ml) grape seed oil

1 cup (250 ml) extra virgin olive oil

Salt and freshly ground black pepper

### SALSA:

1 tomato, seeded and diced

12 black olives, halved

5 sweet gherkin pickles, julienned

3 tbsp (45 ml) small capers

2-3 tbsp (30-45 ml) olive oil

1 lemon, peeled and cut into sections

Juice of 1 lemon

1 tbsp (15 ml) chopped chives

5 basil leaves, chopped

Salt and freshly ground black pepper

### SALAD:

1 large endive

4 tbsp (60 ml) pine nuts, roasted

½ red onion, julienned

10 coriander leaves

10 cherry tomatoes, halved

7 tbsp (105 ml) extra virgin olive oil

7 tbsp (105 ml) white or red wine vinegar

Salt and freshly ground black pepper

1 avocado

Chives, roughly chopped, for garnish

To prepare emulsion, boil peppercorns in fresh water for 45 minutes. Place boiled peppercorns, pine nuts, grape seed oil, olive oil, salt and pepper in blender and blend until emulsified. Add water if mixture appears too thick. Transfer to a bowl and refrigerate. If emulsion separates, blend again until creamy. Make salsa by mixing all the ingredients together in a bowl. Refrigerate.

To prepare salad, separate endive leaves and remove heart. Cut leaves in half lengthwise. Place in medium-size bowl along with pine nuts, red onion, coriander and cherry tomatoes. Make vinaigrette by mixing together the oil, vinegar, salt and pepper. Just before serving, toss salad with vinaigrette. Prepare avocado by slicing in half lengthwise around pit. Separate the halves, remove skin and remove pit. Slice avocado into long, thin slices and fan out over 4 plates.

Heat grill to high. Grill salmon to desired doneness. To assemble before serving, top avocado slices with salad. Arrange salmon filets on salad and top with salsa. Drizzle plates with emulsion.

Note: To roast pine nuts, place on a baking sheet in oven heated to 350°F (180°C) for 5-7 minutes or until lightly golden.

Serves 4

*Serving Size (296g), Calories 530, Total Fat 39g, Saturated Fat 5g, Cholesterol 95mg, Sodium 500mg, Total Carbohydrate 12g, Dietary Fiber 2g, Sugars 7g, Protein 35g*

SUGGESTED WINE PAIRING:

*Belleruche*
CÔTES-DU-RHÔNE

M. CHAPOUTIER

Chapoutier Belleruche
Represented by:
Vins Philippe Dandurand inc.

# Fish in cartoccio

1 tbsp (15 ml) olive oil

1 filet orange roughy

Salt and freshly ground black pepper

1 tomato, sliced

½ small red onion, sliced

1 garlic clove, minced

Pinch each oregano and basil

¼ cup (65 ml) white wine

Lemon slices and chives for garnish

Heat oven to 400°F (200°C). Cut a 20x20-inch (50x50 cm) piece of parchment paper (or foil). Drizzle most of the olive oil in middle of paper. Season fish with salt and pepper and place on top of oil. Place tomato and onion slices over fish. Sprinkle with garlic, oregano and basil. Drizzle with remaining oil and pour wine over everything. Fold paper around fish to make a packet. Place on a cooking tray and bake for 15 minutes.

Substitution: Any white fish can replace the orange roughy.

Serves 1

*Serving Size (404g), Calories 320, Total Fat 15g, Saturated Fat 2g, Cholesterol 35mg, Sodium 125mg, Total Carbohydrate 11g, Dietary Fiber 2g, Sugars 6g, Protein 27g*

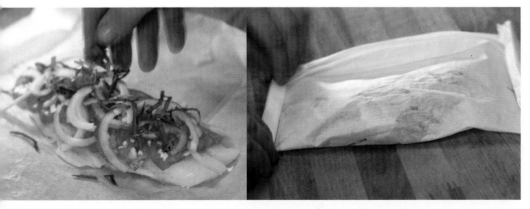

SUGGESTED WINE PAIRING:

CORVO

Sicilia

Corvo Bianco i.g.t. Duca di Salaparuta
Offered by: Italvine

# Filet of tilapia

4 7-oz (200 g) tilapia filets, skin removed

Salt and freshly ground black pepper

Paprika

4 tbsp (60 ml) olive oil plus extra for drizzling

Sprigs of parsley for garnish

FRUIT SALSA:

7 oz (200 g) pineapple, cubed

4 oz (115 g) strawberries, cubed

4 oz (115 g) kiwi, cubed

½ red or white onion, chopped

1 tomato, cubed

1 bunch parsley, chopped (leaving aside a few sprigs for garnish)

2 tbsp (30 ml) red wine vinegar

2 tbsp (30 ml) olive oil

1 tbsp (15 ml) honey

Salt and freshly ground black pepper

In a medium-size bowl, combine pineapple, strawberries, kiwi, onion, tomato and parsley. Add red wine vinegar, olive oil, honey, salt and pepper. Toss together until well mixed.

Heat grill to medium-high. Season fish with salt, pepper and paprika. Drizzle with olive oil. Place on grill and cook 5 minutes on each side. Remove from heat when fish is flaky and tender. Serve tilapia topped with fruit salsa and garnished with parsley sprigs.

Serves 4

*Serving Size (334g), Calories 400, Total Fat 20g, Saturated Fat 3g, Cholesterol 110mg, Sodium 120mg, Total Carbohydrate 21g, Dietary Fiber 3g, Sugars 16g, Protein 34g*

*Martin Brodeur*
*"I'm a big fish lover, and the tilapia with fruit salsa from Prima Luna is simple, healthy and delicious."*

SUGGESTED WINE PAIRING:

MÂCON-VILLAGES
APPELLATION MÂCON-VILLAGES CONTRÔLÉE

CHARDONNAY

GEORGES DUBŒUF

MIS EN BOUTEILLE EN FRANCE PAR · BOTTLED IN FRANCE BY
LES VINS GEORGES DUBŒUF À 71570 ROMANÈCHE-THORINS FRANCE
PRODUCT OF FRANCE · PRODUIT DE FRANCE

Duboeuf Mâcon-Villages
Chardonnay
Represented by:
Vins Philippe Dandurand inc.

Fruit salsa

Halibut

# Cinnamon-scented halibut, red beets and spinach in a white wine and port sauce

cuisine inspirée

½ cup (125 ml) red port wine

1 tbsp (15 ml) sugar (optional)

8 oz (225 g) red beets

4 7-oz (200 g) halibut filets, skin removed

4 tbsp (60 ml) ground cinnamon

1 tbsp (15 ml) olive oil

1 tbsp (15 ml) butter

2 cups (500 ml) baby spinach

Salt and freshly ground black pepper

Cinnamon stick for garnish

BEURRE BLANC SAUCE:

2 tsp (10 ml) shallots, chopped

1 tbsp (15 ml) olive oil

¼ cup (65 ml) white wine

2 cups (500 ml) fish stock

Pinch each thyme and laurel

Salt and freshly ground black pepper

1 tbsp (15 ml) butter, cold

Heat port in a small pot on low until reduced by about 85%. It should have the consistency of a syrup. Add sugar to make more syrupy, if desired. Set aside. In a separate pot, boil beets in salted water until tender. Drain and let cool slightly. Wearing rubber gloves to avoid staining your hands, rub beets to remove skins. When completely cool, scoop beets into small balls using a melon baller. Set aside.

To prepare *beurre blanc* sauce, heat oil in heavy frying pan over high heat. Add shallots and sauté until browned. Deglaze with white wine and allow liquid to almost evaporate. Add fish stock, thyme and laurel. Simmer sauce over low to reduce by half. While still hot, pass through a cheesecloth and season with salt and pepper. Keep warm in pan. Just before serving, add cold butter to sauce and whisk quickly until creamy and completely emulsified.

Rub fish on one side with cinnamon. In a separate frying pan, heat oil over high heat. Add fish cinnamon side down and cook until crispy. Flip over and turn heat to low. Continue cooking until fish is flaky and tender. In a third pan, melt butter over medium-high heat and sauté spinach until limp. Season with salt and pepper and drain on paper towel. Before serving, brush plates with emulsified sauce. Place piece of fish on each plate and accompany with spinach and beets on the side. Drizzle port reduction onto plate for decoration. Garnish fish with cinnamon stick.

Substitution: Striped sea bass, skin on, can be used instead of halibut.

Serves 4

*Serving Size (455g), Calories 420, Total Fat 18g, Saturated Fat 6g, Cholesterol 100mg, Sodium 440mg, Total Carbohydrate 15g, Dietary Fiber 6g, Sugars 7g, Protein 41g*

# Codfish on a bed of green asparagus and virgin sauce

1 bunch asparagus, trimmed

2 cups (500 ml) cherry tomatoes, quartered

1 bunch fresh basil, julienned

¼ cup (65 ml) olive oil plus extra for drizzling

2 tbsp (30 ml) balsamic vinegar

Juice of 2 lemons

Salt and freshly ground black pepper

4 fresh cod filets

Heat oven to 350°F (180°C). Place asparagus on cooking sheet. Drizzle with olive oil and sprinkle with salt. Cook in oven for 10 minutes (after removing asparagus, keep same oven temperature for cod). Meanwhile, prepare virgin sauce by mixing tomatoes, basil, olive oil, vinegar, lemon juice, salt and pepper in a bowl. Set aside.

Heat ¼ cup (65 ml) olive oil in ovenproof frying pan on high. Score filets on both sides. Place in hot pan and sear on one side only. Immediately put pan in oven and cook fish for about 6 minutes, until tender. To serve, place fish seared side up on bed of asparagus and drizzle with virgin sauce.

Substitution: Swordfish, tilapia or red tuna can be used instead of codfish.

Serves 4

*Serving Size (449g), Calories 360, Total Fat 15g, Saturated Fat 2g, Cholesterol 100mg, Sodium 130mg, Total Carbohydrate 11g, Dietary Fiber 3g, Sugars 4g, Protein 43g*

SUGGESTED WINE PAIRING:

COLBARACA

MASI

Soave Classico Colbaraca Masi
Represented by: Maxxium

# Grilled red mullet with truffled panzanella

**Cavalli**
RISTORANTE + BAR

2.2 lbs (1 kg) red mullet

1 tbsp (15 ml) porcini powder

2 tbsp (30 ml) fennel seeds, toasted

2 tbsp (30 ml) coriander seeds, toasted

Salt and freshly ground black pepper

PANZANELLA:

3 vine-ripened tomatoes, diced

1 stalk celery, diced

1 large shallot, diced

2 garlic cloves, chopped

2 oz (60 g) black olives, chopped

2 anchovies packed in oil, diced

1 tsp (5 ml) each chopped basil, parsley and mint

6 tbsp (90 ml) extra virgin olive oil

3 tbsp (45 ml) red wine vinegar

½ cup (125 ml) croutons

---

Heat grill to high. Prepare *panzanella* by mixing all ingredients together in a bowl. Let sit for 5 minutes. In the meantime, place porcini powder, fennel and coriander in a spice grinder and grind until fine. Season fish with spice mixture, salt and pepper. Grill for 2 minutes per side. Serve *panzanella* over fish.

Suggested side dishes: steamed basmati rice and a mix of sautéed baby fennel, asparagus and porcini mushrooms.

Substitution: Red snapper can be used instead of mullet.

Serves 4

*Red Mullet: Serving Size (257g), Calories 280, Total Fat 4.5g, Saturated Fat 1g, Cholesterol 90mg, Sodium 160mg, Total Carbohydrate 4g, Dietary Fiber 3g, Sugars 0g, Protein 53g*
*Truffled Panzanella: Serving Size (184g), Calories 300, Total Fat 26g, Saturated Fat 3.5g, Cholesterol 20mg, Sodium 980mg, Total Carbohydrate 10g, Dietary Fiber 2g, Sugars 3g, Protein 8g*

SUGGESTED WINE PAIRING:

SEDÀRA

DONNAFUGATA

IGT delle Sicilia
Sedara Donnafugata
Represented by: Maxxium

# Seafood cataplana

1¼ lbs (570 g) lobster, tail and claws

1 cup (250 ml) white wine

1 cup (250 ml) tomatoes, peeled and chopped, or 1 cup (250 ml) tomato sauce

1 tbsp (15 ml) olive oil

6 3-oz (85 g) pieces assorted fish such as salmon, halibut, swordfish or mahi-mahi

8 large shrimps, peeled and deveined

6 littleneck clams

6 mussels

2 scallops

2 oz (60 g) Chorizo sausage

4 small potatoes, cooked and halved

½ Spanish onion, finely chopped

2 garlic cloves, minced

½ red pepper, finely chopped

½ yellow pepper, finely chopped

½ green pepper, finely chopped

1 bay leaf

1 tsp (5 ml) piri-piri (hot sauce)

Sea salt and freshly ground black pepper

1 tsp (5 ml) chopped parsley

---

In a large pot, bring 2 cups (500 ml) water, white wine and 1 tsp (5 ml) sea salt to a boil. Add lobster and cook for 8 minutes. Remove lobster from pot, add tomatoes to liquid and continue cooking to make lobster broth.

Heat olive oil in *cataplana* – a round, covered casserole that resembles a wok – over medium heat. Stir in assorted fish, shrimps, clams, mussels, scallops, sausage, potatoes and vegetables. Add lobster broth, bay leaf, piri-piri, salt and pepper. Place lobster, still in shell, on top and cover. Turn heat to high and cook for 6 minutes (clams and mussels should open; if they don't, discard them). Sprinkle with parsley in the last minute of cooking.

Serves 4

*Serving Size (637g), Calories 440, Total Fat 13g, Saturated Fat 3g, Cholesterol 200mg, Sodium 1080mg, Total Carbohydrate 16g, Dietary Fiber 3g, Sugars 4g, Protein 53g*

SUGGESTED WINE PAIRING:

FOLONARI

SOAVE

Folonari Soave - White
Represented by:
Vins Philippe Dandurand inc.

Spanish
onions

# Bakaliaro plaki
## Dry Codfish

2 sides salted codfish, about 4.4 lbs (2 kg)

15 potatoes, washed and peeled

3 28-oz (840 g) cans whole tomatoes, crushed by hand

1 fennel bulb, stem removed, thinly sliced

3 large Vidalia onions, diced

7 garlic cloves, minced

1 cup (250 ml) chopped parsley

1½ tbsp (22 ml) freshly ground black pepper

1 cup (250 ml) olive oil

2 bay leaves

Sprig of thyme for garnish

Soak cod in water for 24 hours, changing water every 8 hours. Remove from water and rinse thoroughly. Slice fish into 5-oz (160 g) portions. If ends of fish are very thick, slice in half lengthwise so portions are uniform.

Heat oven to 350°F (180°C). Prepare potatoes by cutting into ¼-inch (6 mm) slices. Layer bottom of casserole with potatoes and arrange fish portions on top. In large bowl, mix together tomatoes, fennel, parsley, onions, garlic, pepper and olive oil. Spread tomato mixture evenly over fish. Add bay leaves. Cover casserole with foil and bake for 1½ hours. Before serving, garnish with fresh thyme.

Serves 8 to 10

*Serving Size (631g) Calories 610, Total Fat 28g, Saturated Fat 4g, Cholesterol 75mg, Sodium 250mg, Total Carbohydrate 58g, Dietary Fiber 8g, Sugars 11g, Protein 40g*

# Bloody Caesar salmon

GLOBE

12 littleneck or pasta clams

4 4-oz (115 g) salmon filets, deboned

2 tbsp (30 ml) canola oil

4 tbsp (60 ml) vodka

12 Roma tomatoes, peeled, seeded and diced

1 celery heart, finely chopped

2-4 celery leaves plus extra for garnish

½ cup (125 ml) Clamato juice

2 drops Worcestershire

2 drops Tabasco

Salt and freshly ground black pepper

Chives for garnish


POACHED TOMATOES:

16 cherry tomatoes

Olive oil

Poach cherry tomatoes by placing in a pot and just covering with olive oil. Simmer over very low heat for about 10 minutes. Remove tomatoes from oil and set aside. Oil may be stored for future use.

Rinse clams well under cold water. Place in a pot, cover with water and boil until shells open. Remove from liquid and set aside. Discard liquid and clams that didn't open.

Season both sides of salmon filets with salt and pepper. Add canola oil to frying pan and place over medium heat. Cook salmon filets for about 3 minutes per side or until cooked through. Remove and set aside. Pour off excess oil from pan and return to medium heat. Using wooden spoon, deglaze pan with vodka for about 2 seconds. Stir in tomatoes, celery and celery leaves. Add Clamato, Worcestershire and Tabasco. Season with salt and pepper to taste. Reduce mixture by simmering for about 10 minutes. Add cooked clams.

While reducing, place salmon filets in oven at low temperature to warm up. Arrange salmon on plates and top with tomato-clam mixture. Garnish with poached tomatoes, celery leaves and chives.

Serves 4

*Serving Size (584g), Calories 410, Total Fat 17g, Saturated Fat 2g, Cholesterol 90mg, Sodium 230mg, Total Carbohydrate 22g, Dietary Fiber 4g, Sugars 12g, Protein 37g*

142

# Salmon, summer squash and lemon-basil emulsion

4 salmon filets, 6-8 oz (170-225 g) each

Salt and freshly ground black pepper

1 tbsp (15 ml) olive oil

1 green zucchini, julienned

1 yellow zucchini, julienned

1 celery root, julienned

1 leek, julienned

½ tsp (2 ml) salt

Freshly ground black pepper

LEMON-BASIL EMULSION:

½ cup (125 ml) lemon juice

1 tbsp (15 ml) butter, softened

½ tsp (2 ml) sugar

¼ tsp (1 ml) salt

Small bunch basil

To prepare emulsion, place lemon juice in a small pot over medium heat and reduce by half. In a blender, add reduced lemon juice to butter, sugar, basil and salt and purée until smooth.

Season salmon with salt and pepper and grill or poach according to your preference. Heat oil in frying pan over medium-high heat and sauté zucchini, celery root and leek until tender, about 2-4 minutes. Season with salt and pepper. To serve, arrange vegetables in the center of each plate, top with salmon and drizzle with lemon-basil emulsion.

Serves 4

*Salmon: Serving Size (308g), Calories 360, Total Fat 16g, Saturated Fat 2.5g, Cholesterol 105mg, Sodium 460mg, Total Carbohydrate 13g, Dietary Fiber 3g, Sugars 3g, Protein 41g*
*Emulsion: Serving Size (30g), Calories 25, Total Fat 2g, Saturated Fat 1g, Cholesterol 5mg, Sodium 115mg, Total Carbohydrate 2g, Dietary Fiber 0g, Sugars 1g, Protein 0g*

# Meat & Poultry

# Roast chicken breast with warm potato salad and mustard vinaigrette

taverne
SUR LE
SQUARE

8 new potatoes, quartered

Handful green beans, whole

4 bone-in chicken breasts, skin on

Salt and freshly ground black pepper

1 tbsp (15 ml) oil

Assorted greens such as arugula, endive and baby spinach

12 cherry tomatoes, halved

PICKLED VEGETABLES:

2 cups (500 ml) cider vinegar

1 cup (250 ml) red wine vinegar

1 cup (250 ml) water

1 cup (250 ml) sugar

1 tbsp (15 ml) coarse salt

1 tbsp (15 ml) pickling spice

2 red onions, julienned

2 bell peppers, julienned

VINAIGRETTE:

½ cup (125 ml) Pommery mustard

¾ cup (190 ml) olive oil

½ cup (125 ml) red wine vinegar

2 garlic cloves

2 shallots, chopped

1½ tbsp (22 ml) salt

1 tbsp (15 ml) pepper

1½ tbsp (22 ml) sugar

The pickled vegetables must be made a day in advance. Place cider vinegar, red wine vinegar, water, sugar, salt and pickling spice into a large pot and bring to a boil. Place peppers and onions in separate containers. Strain pickling liquid over peppers and onions until submerged. Let sit 1 day in the refrigerator, covered. Discard remaining liquid.

Prepare vinaigrette by blending mustard, olive oil, red wine vinegar, garlic, shallots, salt, pepper and sugar in a blender until emulsified.

In a pot of salted water, boil potatoes until just tender. Remove from water and keep warm. Using a separate pot with fresh salted water, boil green beans for 3 minutes. Drain and place in ice bath to prevent overcooking. Drain again when cooled.

To prepare chicken, heat oven to 400°F (200°C). Season chicken with salt and pepper. Heat a heavy, non-stick, ovenproof frying pan to hot. Add oil, then chicken breast, skin side down. When skin has browned, place pan in oven. Cook 10-13 minutes, then turn chicken over and continue cooking for 3-5 minutes more, depending on thickness of chicken. To serve, arrange greens and cherry tomatoes over 4 plates and place chicken on top. Serve with potatoes, green beans and pickled vegetables. Drizzle with vinaigrette.

Note: Both the vinaigrette and pickling liquid will keep well in the refrigerator if stored in a covered container, the former for 2 weeks, the latter for 2-3 weeks.

Serves 4

*Chicken: Serving Size (373g), Calories 390, Total Fat 14g, Saturated Fat 4g, Cholesterol 95mg, Sodium 430mg, Total Carbohydrate 32g, Dietary Fiber 5g, Sugars 2g, Protein 34g*

*Pickled Vegetables: Serving Size (300g), Calories 300, Total Fat 1g, Saturated Fat 0g, Cholesterol 0mg, Sodium 70mg, Total Carbohydrate 25g, Dietary Fiber 8g, Sugars 24g, Protein 5g*

*Vinaigrette: Serving Size (65g), Calories 210, Total Fat 20g, Saturated Fat 2.5g, Cholesterol 0mg, Sodium 1670mg, Total Carbohydrate 4g, Dietary Fiber 0g, Sugars 3g, Protein 0g*

chicken

# Seared duck breast
## with port raspberry sauce

2 whole magret duck breasts, 1 lb (450 g) each

Salt and freshly ground black pepper

3 oz (90 ml) dry red wine

3 oz (90 ml) duck or chicken stock

3 oz (90 ml) port wine

¾ cup (190 ml) raspberries

CREAMY POLENTA:

2 cups (500 ml) 2% milk

1 cup (250 ml) 10% cream

5 garlic cloves, whole

5 large fresh basil leaves

1 cup (250 ml) polenta fina (fine cornmeal)

Salt and freshly ground black pepper

Make polenta by bringing milk, cream (may be replaced with 2% milk), garlic cloves and basil to a boil in a heavy pot. Reduce heat to medium and let simmer for 10 minutes. With a slotted spoon, remove garlic and basil. Reduce heat to low and add polenta. Continue stirring while mixture is cooking, about 5-10 minutes. Polenta is ready when mixture is thick, soft and creamy. Add salt and pepper to taste.

To prepare duck, trim fat evenly to ¼ inch (0.5 cm) and score in a criss-cross pattern. Generously season both sides of duck with salt and pepper. Heat frying pan over medium heat and add duck, breast side down. Cook until fat is golden-brown, about 8 minutes. Turn breasts over and sauté for another 4 minutes, until meat is rare to medium-rare. Transfer to plate and cover with foil. Let duck rest while preparing sauce.

Pour the fat from pan and return to heat. Using a wooden spoon, deglaze pan while adding red wine. Add stock, port and raspberries and reduce liquid mixture by a third. To serve duck, slice on bias, arrange on top of creamy polenta and drizzle generously with sauce.

Suggested side dish: sautéed spinach.

Serves 4

*Duck Breast: Serving Size (316g), Calories 340, Total Fat 10g, Saturated Fat 3g, Cholesterol 175mg, Sodium 200mg, Total Carbohydrate 6g, Dietary Fiber 2g, Sugars 4g, Protein 45g*

*Creamy Polenta: Serving Size (113g), Calories 160, Total Fat 6g, Saturated Fat 4g, Cholesterol 25mg, Sodium 45mg, Total Carbohydrate 21g, Dietary Fiber 2g, Sugars 3g, Protein 5g*

SUGGESTED WINE PAIRING:

MIS EN BOUTEILLE AU DOMAINE · ESTATE BOTTLED

**COUSIÑO-MACUL**

**ANTIGUAS RESERVAS**
Cabernet Sauvignon 2004

D.O. VALLE DEL MAIPO

RED CHILEAN WINE · VIN ROUGE DU CHILI

750 ml                    12% alc./vol.

Cousino-Macul Cabernet Sauvignon
Antiguas Reservas
Represented by:
Vins Philippe Dandurand inc.

# New York carpet bag

2 oz (55 g) wild mushroom mix such as chanterelle, oyster, king or shitake

8 oz (225 g) aged New York strip loin steak

2 tbsp (30 ml) grape seed oil

2 garlic cloves, minced

Pinch each fresh chervil, thyme and rosemary

Salt and freshly ground pepper

½ cup (125 ml) port wine

Steak spice for garnish

¼ cup (65 ml) veal stock (optional)

2 tbsp (30 ml) 35% cream (optional)

Prepare broiler or grill at high heat. Clean mushrooms with small brush, removing excess soil, and let stand under cold running water. Pat dry, then slice lengthwise.

Place steak on broiler or grill and cook for 4 minutes per side for medium rare. Meanwhile, heat grape seed oil in cast iron pan over medium-high heat. Add garlic, chervil, thyme, rosemary, salt and pepper. Add mushrooms to pan and sauté for 3 minutes. Add port and stir to deglaze. Reduce liquid by half and remove from heat.

When steak is cooked, remove from broiler or grill and let sit for several minutes. Slice while still warm. To serve, divide mushrooms between 2 plates, top with sliced steak and drizzle with reduction. Garnish with steak spice, if desired.

Suggested side dish: roasted butternut squash or mashed Yukon Gold potatoes.

Option: Combine veal stock and cream and add to mushroom reduction. Season with salt and pepper to taste. Cook another 2 minutes.

Serves 1

*Mushroom Sauce: Serving Size (30g), Calories 35, Total Fat 3.5g, Saturated Fat 2.5g, Cholesterol 15mg, Sodium 80mg, Total Carbohydrate 0g, Dietary Fiber 0g, Sugars 0g, Protein 0g*

*NY Carpet Bag: Serving Size (217g), Calories 610, Total Fat 43g, Saturated Fat 13g, Cholesterol 90mg, Sodium 75mg, Total Carbohydrate 9g, Dietary Fiber 0g, Sugars 7g, Protein 29g*

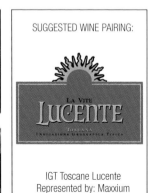

*Otis Grant*

*"If you're looking for elegance, class and style with a fantastic ambiance and terrific service, you need look no further than 40 Westt Steakhouse & Rawbar. It will knock you out!"*

SUGGESTED WINE PAIRING:

LA VITE
LUCENTE
TOSCANA

IGT Toscane Lucente
Represented by: Maxxium

# Brasato di stinco d'agnello
## Braised lamb shanks
## with anchovy and tomatoes

6 small lamb shanks

2 tbsp (30 ml) extra virgin olive oil

Salt and freshly ground black pepper

6 anchovy filets

2 garlic cloves, thinly sliced

1 tbsp (15 ml) fresh rosemary, chopped

1 small dried red chili pepper, crushed

½ cup (125 ml) dry white wine

1½ cups (375 ml) beef or lamb stock

1 cup (250 ml) fresh or canned tomatoes, peeled, seeded and chopped

¾ cup (190 ml) Gaeta black olives

1 tbsp (15 ml) chopped Italian parsley

Fresh rosemary for garnish

Pat lamb shanks dry. In a heavy frying pan large enough to hold shanks in a single layer, warm olive oil over medium heat. Add shanks and cook until well browned on all sides, about 15 minutes. Spoon off any accumulated fat.

Sprinkle shanks with salt and pepper. Add anchovies, garlic, rosemary and chili peppers and cook for 1 minute. Pour in wine and bring to a simmer. Add beef stock and tomatoes. Reduce heat to low and cover. Simmer shanks, turning occasionally, until meat is tender, about 1½ hours. Stir in olives and heat through. Arrange on warmed platter. Before serving, sprinkle with fresh rosemary.

Suggested side dish: plain polenta.

Serves 6

Serving Size (267g), Calories 360, Total Fat 18g, Saturated Fat 3.5g, Cholesterol 110mg, Sodium 1850mg,
Total Carbohydrate 8g, Dietary Fiber-less than 1g, Sugars 2g, Protein 37g

SUGGESTED WINE PAIRING:

BROLIO

2003 CHIANTI CLASSICO BARONE RICASOLI

Ricasoli Brolio
Represented by:
Vins Philippe Dandurand inc.

# Bison two ways: roasted loin and braised short ribs

LE CLUB
CHASSE
et PÊCHE

**BRAISED SHORT RIBS:**

4 strips bison short ribs, about 3 lbs (1.5 kg)
1 tbsp (15 ml) oil
1 cup (250 ml) red wine
4 cups (1 l) game or veal stock
Slab lean smoked bacon, 1x1x4 inches
(2.5x2.5x10 cm)
5-6 whole black peppercorns
1 bunch each thyme, parsley and chives
2 bay leaves
Fleur de sel

**MIREPOIX:**

1 carrot
1 celery stalk
1 leek, whites only
1 onion
2 sprigs each thyme and parsley
Pinch fresh chives

4 large Jerusalem artichokes, peeled
2 tbsp (30 ml) butter

**BERRY SAUCE:**

2 cups (500 ml) each blueberries,
blackberries and raspberries

1 garlic clove, sliced in half
¼ carrot, finely diced
1½ cups (375 ml) sliced shallots
1 cup (250 ml) sugar
½ tsp (2 ml) freshly ground black pepper
1 cup (250 ml) Zinfandel vinegar
1½ cups (375 ml) Zinfandel red wine
8 cups (2 l) brown game or veal demi-glace

**ROASTED LOIN:**

1 tbsp (15 ml) butter
1½ lbs (675 g) bison loin
1-2 tbsp (15-30 ml) extra virgin olive oil
1 lb (450 g) baby spinach, sautéed and drained

SHORT RIBS: Cook 1 day in advance. Cut strips into individual ribs. Place oil in a large, heavy frying pan over high heat. When hot, sear ribs on all sides until well caramelized. Pour off fat. Deglaze pan with red wine, stirring to incorporate brown bits. Transfer ribs to heavy casserole. Add stock, bacon, peppercorns, herbs, bay leaves, *fleur de sel* and *mirepoix* ingredients. Over medium-high heat, bring mixture to a boil. Remove from stovetop and cover tightly. Roast in oven heated to 250°F (130°C) for 12 hours. Allow ribs to cool, then remove from liquid, cover and refrigerate. Discard liquid.

Make berry sauce by bringing all ingredients except red wine and demi-glace to a boil. Continue cooking until liquid is reduced by half. Add red wine and reduce by two thirds. Add demi-glace and let simmer until thick enough to coat the back of a spoon. Remove from heat.

To make Jerusalem artichokes, heat oven to 400°F (200°C). In a frying pan on medium-high, cook in butter until golden. Remove from heat. Place on baking tray and cook for a few minutes, until tender. Set aside.

LOIN: Using heavy frying pan, sear loin in oil over high heat on all sides until medium-rare. Let meat rest for 10-15 minutes before slicing. Arrange on serving plate and drizzle plate with berry sauce.

To finish ribs, heat oven to 400°F (200°C). Place meaty side down in oven-proof dish and cover with berry sauce. Cook in oven for 12-15 minutes or until hot. To serve both dishes, gently crush Jerusalem artichokes and arrange in desired shape. Top with glazed ribs. On same plate, arrange sautéed spinach, drizzle with olive oil and season with *fleur de sel*. Lay sliced loin over spinach. Drizzle plate with berry sauce.

Serves 4

*Short Ribs: Serving Size (342g), Calories 710, Total Fat 58g,
Saturated Fat 23g, Cholesterol 115mg, Sodium 240mg,
Total Carbohydrate 20g, Dietary Fiber 5g, Sugars 4g, Protein 29g*

*Loin: Serving Size (370g), Calories 340, Total Fat 13g,
Saturated Fat 3.5g, Cholesterol 95mg, Sodium 260mg,
Total Carbohydrate 20g, Dietary Fiber 5g, Sugars 4g, Protein 336g*

*Berry Sauce: Serving Size (30g), Calories 15, Total Fat 0g,
Saturated Fat 0g, Cholesterol 0mg, Sodium 60mg,
Total Carbohydrate 3g, Dietary Fiber 0g, Sugars 2g, Protein 0g*

# Grilled chicken with La Louisiane spice mix

**SPICE MIX:**

½ cup (125 ml) paprika

¼ cup (65 ml) garlic powder

¼ cup (65 ml) onion powder

2 tbsp (30 ml) cayenne pepper

2 tbsp (30 ml) white pepper

2 tbsp (30 ml) black pepper

2 tbsp (30 ml) dried basil

2 tbsp (30 ml) dried thyme

2 tbsp (30 ml) dried oregano

2 tbsp (30 ml) salt

Mix all the spices together in a bowl. Coat boneless chicken breasts with seasoning and grill until done. Serve with a fresh salad.

Note: This seasoning also works well with fish, pork and beef, or anything else you like to grill.

*Serving Size (170g), Calories 190, Total Fat 2g, Saturated Fat 0.5g, Cholesterol 100mg, Sodium 110mg, Total Carbohydrate 0g, Dietary Fiber 0g, Sugars 0g, Protein 39g*

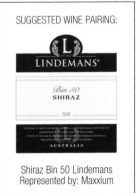

SUGGESTED WINE PAIRING:

**LINDEMANS**

*Bin 50*
SHIRAZ

AUSTRALIA

Shiraz Bin 50 Lindemans
Represented by: Maxxium

# Filet of pork
## and sweet potato purée

2 pork filets

2 sweet potatoes, peeled and cubed

1 envelope commercial demi-glace

2 tbsp (30 ml) olive oil

1 tbsp (15 ml) plus 1 tsp (5 ml) maple syrup

2 drops vanilla

Chives for garnish

Salt and freshly ground black pepper

Boil potatoes until tender. Drain and mash into a purée, along with 1 tbsp (15 ml) of the olive oil, 1 drop of the vanilla, 1 tsp (5 ml) of the maple syrup and salt and pepper. Set aside.

Heat oven to 400°F (200°C). Season pork filets with salt and pepper to taste. In a heavy frying pan heated to high, add remaining olive oil and sear both sides of filets. Continue cooking in oven until done to your taste. In the meantime, prepare demi-glace according to package instructions. Add 1 drop vanilla and remaining maple syrup. To serve, cut each filet diagonally into 4 pieces and arrange 2 pieces on each plate. Accompany with a serving of sweet potato purée. Top meat with sauce.

Suggested side dish: assorted steamed vegetables.

Serves 4

*Serving Size (205g), Calories 370, Total Fat 15g, Saturated Fat 4g, Cholesterol 95mg, Sodium 360mg, Total Carbohydrates 22g, Dietary Fiber 2g, Sugars 10g, Protein 36g*

SUGGESTED WINE PAIRING:

ROSEMOUNT
SOUTH EASTERN AUSTRALIA
PINOT NOIR
750 mL

Pinot Noir Diamond Label
Rosemount Estate
Represented by: Maxxium

# Filet mignon with scallops
## over braised leeks

4 10-oz (290 g) cuts of filet mignon

4 leeks, julienned

2 tbsp (30 ml) butter

4 scallops

8 slices bacon

4 tsp (20 ml) cognac

Salt and freshly ground 5-pepper mix

Heat grill to high. Drizzle cognac over bacon slices. Sprinkle with pepper. Wrap 2 slices bacon around each filet. Season lightly with salt. Cook filets 6-7 minutes for medium-rare and 2 minutes more for medium, flipping halfway through. Season filets with additional pepper 1 minute before removing from grill.

While meat is grilling, steam julienned leeks for 45 seconds or until tender. Heat frying pan to high and sauté steamed leeks in half the butter for about 3 minutes. Remove from pan. In same skillet, still on high, sear scallops in remaining butter for about 3 minutes per side. Season with salt and pepper. To serve, arrange leeks on plate next to filet mignon and top with scallop.

Serves 4

*Serving Size (446g), Calories 690, Total Fat 35g, Saturated Fat 15g, Cholesterol 225mg, Sodium 970mg, Total Carbohydrate 14g, Dietary Fiber 2g, Sugars 4g, Protein 74g*

SUGGESTED WINE PAIRING:

Cabernet Sauvignon
BIN 407 Penfolds
Represented by: Maxxium

163

# Slow-roasted rack of organic piglet

2 racks of piglet

6 tbsp (90 ml) olive oil plus extra for garnish

Salt and freshly ground black pepper

14 oz (400 g) fresh spinach

1 tbsp (15 ml) chili pepper

1 cup (250 ml) vegetable stock

3 tbsp (45 ml) Riesling

Assorted vegetables such as carrots, parsnips, corn, sweet peas and wild mushrooms, peeled if necessary and diced

4 tbsp (60 ml) chopped mixed fresh herbs such as thyme, rosemary, parsley, chervil and lovage

Heat oven to 300°F (150°C). Place racks of meat on cooking tray and drizzle with most of the olive oil. Season to taste with salt and pepper. Roast meat for about 20 minutes or according to your taste, occasionally turning it over and brushing with olive oil. Remove from oven and let stand for 10 minutes before slicing.

While meat is cooking, bring a large pot of water to a boil. Add spinach and cook quickly. Drain and submerge in cold water to prevent further cooking. Drain again. Purée spinach in food processor with chili pepper. Add a bit of water if necessary. Keep hot.

In a second large pot, bring stock and wine to a boil. Drop in vegetables. Cover, reduce heat to low and cook for about 5 minutes. Drain vegetables and set aside in a warm place, returning liquid to pot to make a reduction. When liquid has been reduced over low heat to desired consistency, add mixed herbs to taste.

To serve, arrange spinach purée on half of serving dish. Top with vegetable stew. Place sliced meat next to vegetables and drizzle with reduction and olive oil.

Serves 4

*Serving Size (426g), Calories 620, Total Fat 46g, Saturated Fat 11g, Cholesterol 100mg, Sodium 950mg, Total Carbohydrate 10g, Dietary Fiber 5g, Sugars 4g, Protein 38g*

SUGGESTED WINE PAIRING:

Fontanafredda Barbera D'Alba
Represented by: Whitehall Agencies

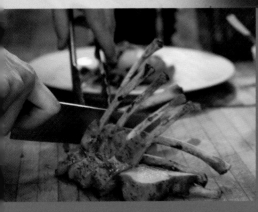

# Parsnips, corn, sweet peas

# Arrosto di Vitello
## Roasted veal

3 tbsp (45 ml) extra virgin olive oil

2 garlic cloves, peeled and smashed

½ lb (225 g) radicchio, chopped

1½ tbsp (22 ml) prosciutto, cut into slivers

Salt and freshly ground black pepper

⅓ cup (85 ml) dry white wine

1½ lbs (675 g) veal tenderloin,
cut into 4 pieces

Sprig of fresh rosemary for garnish

Heat oil in heavy frying pan over high heat. Brown garlic cloves. Add radicchio and prosciutto. Lower heat to medium and cook until tender. Season with salt and pepper to taste. Add wine and cook on low for 2-3 minutes. Using a slotted spoon, remove mixture and set aside, preserving juices in pan.

With heat on high, brown veal in remaining pan juices. Cover and cook on medium-low for 10-15 minutes, until veal is tender. Serve veal topped with radicchio mixture and garnish with rosemary.

Serves 4

*Serving Size (215g), Calories 350, Total Fat 20g, Saturated Fat 5g, Cholesterol 135mg, Sodium 250mg, Total Carbohydrate 3g, Dietary Fiber-less than 1g, Sugars 0g, Protein 34g*

# Rack of lamb

2 racks of lamb

Salt and freshly ground black pepper

1 tomato, diced

1 small garlic clove, minced

Extra virgin olive oil

White balsamic vinegar

1 lemon, peeled and sectioned

1 oz (30 g) feta cheese, crumbled

½ cup (125 ml) black olives

Greek oregano

Fresh mint for garnish

Heat oven to 500°F (260°C). Season lamb with salt and pepper. In a heavy frying pan, sear meat in 2 tbsp (30 ml) of olive oil over high heat until golden-brown. Transfer to ovenproof dish and cook in oven, uncovered, for 15 minutes. Remove and allow meat to rest for 10-15 minutes, uncovered, before slicing.

Mix tomato and garlic together and drizzle with olive oil and white balsamic vinegar. Slice the lamb. Top meat with tomato mixture, lemon sections, feta, black olives and oregano. Drizzle with olive oil. Garnish with fresh mint.

Serves 4

*Serving Size (277g), Calories 340, Total Fat 19g, Saturated Fat 5g, Cholesterol 115mg, Sodium 440mg, Total Carbohydrate 7g, Dietary Fiber 2g, Sugars 2g, Protein 36g*

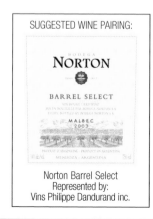

SUGGESTED WINE PAIRING:

Norton Barrel Select
Represented by:
Vins Philippe Dandurand inc.

Vodka

# Caribou filet and wild berry vodka blend, served with a potato gratin and sautéed oyster mushrooms

4 6-oz (170 g) caribou filets

2 tbsp (30 ml) olive oil

6 oyster mushrooms, whole

25 pearl onions

Salt and freshly ground black pepper

Fresh rosemary and thyme for garnish

**POTATO GRATIN:**

1 cup (250 ml) 35% cream

1 tbsp (15 ml) maple syrup

½ bundle chives, chopped

Sprig of thyme, chopped

4 large potatoes, peeled, thinly sliced

½ cup (125 ml) grated Oka cheese

**WILD BERRY BLEND:**

½ cup (125 ml) blueberries

½ tsp (2 ml) Dijon mustard

¼ cup (65 ml) olive oil

2 tbsp (30 ml) vodka

Salt and freshly ground black pepper

To prepare wild berry blend, add all the ingredients to a food processor, blend and set aside.

To prepare potato gratin, heat oven to 350°F (180°C). Place cream, maple syrup, thyme and chives in a small pot over high heat. Cook for a few minutes but do not bring to a boil. Arrange potatoes over bottom of a 5x5-inch (13x13 cm) ovenproof dish. Pour cream-syrup mixture over potatoes and cook in oven for 1 hour. In the last 10 minutes of cooking, top potato-cream mixture with Oka cheese, cover and continue cooking. Let stand while preparing caribou filets.

Heat oven to 400°F (200°C). Add 2 tbsp (30 ml) olive oil to heavy frying pan heated to high. When oil starts to smoke, add caribou and sear both sides. Remove from pan and cook in oven for 10 more minutes or until done to your taste. Remove from oven. Using the same pan, sauté the mushrooms and onions. Add salt and pepper. To serve, spoon potato gratin onto plate and top with mushroom mixture. Place filet over mixture. Drizzle with wild berry blend and garnish with fresh herbs.

Suggested side dish: assorted steamed vegetables.

Serves 4

*Serving Size (840g), Calories 920, Total Fat 48g, Saturated Fat 21g, Cholesterol 240mg, Sodium 320mg, Total Carbohydrate 66g, Dietary Fiber 14g, Sugars 15g, Protein 58g*

SUGGESTED VODKA:

**ABSOLUT** *Country of Sweden* **VODKA**

Absolut Vodka
Represented by: Maxxium

# Honey-glazed, corn-fed chicken with lavender and root vegetables

4 chicken breasts, bone in and skin on

MARINADE:

1 tbsp (15 ml) yellow mustard

¼ tbsp (4 ml) Dijon mustard

2 garlic cloves, minced

2 tbsp (30 ml) olive oil

1 tbsp (15 ml) salt

Freshly ground black pepper

2 sprigs each rosemary and thyme

HONEY GLAZE:

¼ cup (65 ml) honey

Juice of 1 lemon

¼ tbsp (4 ml) lavender water,
or rose or orange blossom water

VEGETABLES:

8 mini carrots, stemmed

8 mini zucchini

8 mini yellow summer squash

4 stalks mini rapini

Mix marinade ingredients together in a freezer bag. Add chicken breasts, cover in marinade and leave in the refrigerator overnight. Prepare honey glaze by mixing all ingredients together in a small bowl. Cover and set aside.

Remove chicken from refrigerator. Heat oven to 350°F (180°C). Using a heavy ovenproof frying pan, heat 1 tbsp (15 ml) of the olive oil on high and sear chicken breasts until browned and crispy. Put pan in oven and cook for 12-15 minutes. Brush chicken with honey glaze in the last 3 minutes of cooking (glaze will burn if added too early).

Steam vegetables. While still firm, drain and transfer to an ovenproof dish. Keep warm in oven for 5-10 minutes while chicken finishes cooking. To serve, arrange chicken and vegetables side by side on a serving plate.

Note: To intensify the flavor, brush chicken with reduced veal stock before serving. Chicken may be grilled instead of seared on stovetop before placing in oven.

Serves 4

*Serving Size (516g), Calories 380, Total Fat 10g, Saturated Fat 1.5g, Cholesterol 100mg, Sodium 130mg, Total Carbohydrate 32g, Dietary Fiber 5g, Sugars 24g, Protein 44g*

SUGGESTED WINE PAIRING:

2005

COL DI SASSO

BANFI

CABERNET SAUVIGNON & SANGIOVESE

Banfi Col di Sasso
Represented by: Charton Hobbs

# Veal filet with roasted vegetable caponata and green olive tapenade

1 8-oz (225 g) veal filet

Salt and freshly ground black pepper

1 tbsp (15 ml) olive oil


VEGETABLE CAPONATA:

1 tbsp (15 ml) olive oil

5 oz (140 g) butternut squash, cubed

5 oz (140 g) celery root, cubed

5 oz (140 g) carrots, diced

2 tsp (10 ml) pine nuts, roasted

2 tsp (10 ml) dry raisins

2 tsp (10 ml) red wine vinegar

Pinch chopped fresh chives

Pinch chopped shallots


GREEN OLIVE TAPENADE:

4 large green olives, pitted

1 tsp (5 ml) olive oil

½ tsp (2 ml) Sambal Olek (chili paste)

½ tsp (2 ml) minced lime zest

½ tsp (2 ml) minced orange zest

Pinch minced shallots

Pinch minced fresh herbs such as basil, mint, thyme or chives


LEMON CONFIT:

Zest of 1 Meyer lemon *(see note below)*

---

Heat grill to high and oven to 400°F (200°C). Season veal with salt and pepper on both sides. Grill meat on all sides to sear. Transfer to ovenproof dish and cook in oven for 10 minutes. Remove and let rest for 7 minutes before slicing.

To prepare *caponata*, heat olive oil in heavy frying pan over high heat and sear squash, celery root and carrots separately. Transfer all vegetables to cooking tray and cook in oven at 400°F (200°C) until tender. In a large bowl, toss with pine nuts, raisins, vinegar, chives and shallots. Set aside. Prepare tapenade by placing olives, olive oil and Sambal Olek in a food processor and processing until roughly chopped. Transfer to a bowl and combine with shallots, lime and orange zest and fresh herbs. To serve, arrange *caponata* on a serving plate and top with sliced veal. Spoon tapenade over veal and garnish with lemon confit.

Note: Meyer lemons, which are sweet and perfect as a garnish, are available only seasonally. To prepare lemon confit with regular lemons, boil lemon zest, drain and repeat 2 more times in fresh water to remove bitterness.

### Serves 2

*Veal: Serving Size (113g), Calories 140, Total Fat 4.5g, Saturated Fat 1.5g, Cholesterol 95mg, Sodium 110mg, Total Carbohydrate 0g, Dietary Fiber 0g, Sugars 0g, Protein 23g*

*Caponata: Serving Size (238g), Calories 240, Total Fat 16g, Saturated Fat 2.5g, Cholesterol 0mg, Sodium 100mg, Total Carbohydrate 24g, Dietary Fiber 6g, Sugars 10g, Protein 3g*

*Tapenade: Serving Size (8.5g), Calories 22.5, Total Fat 2.25g, Saturated Fat 0g, Cholesterol 0mg, Sodium 130mg, Total Carbohydrate 1g, Dietary Fiber 0g, Sugars 0g, Protein 0g*

# Grilled filet mignon on bone

4 bone-in filets, 2 inches (5 cm) thick

1 garlic bulb, roasted with olive oil and thyme

SPICE MIX:

2 tsp (10 ml) ground coriander

1 tsp (5 ml) salt

1 tsp (5 ml) red pepper flakes

2 tsp (10 m) mustard seed

2 tsp (10 ml) ground fennel

2 tsp (10 ml) garlic powder

2 tsp (10 ml) onion flakes

2 tsp (10 ml) freshly ground black pepper

Heat grill to high. Cook filets 2-3 minutes on each side to sear. Reduce heat to low. Cook filets 8-9 minutes on each side for medium-rare. Sprinkle with spice mix 1 minute before removing filets from grill.

Heat oven to 400°F (200°C). To make roasted garlic, slice off pointy end of bulb and drizzle with olive oil. Season with pinch of salt, pepper and thyme. Cook in oven open side up for 20-25 minutes. Before serving filets, place roasted garlic bulb on top.

Serves 4

*Serving Size (187g), Calories 550, Total Fat 38g, Saturated Fat 15g, Cholesterol 160mg, Sodium 110mg, Total Carbohydrate 0g, Dietary Fiber 0g, Sugars 0g, Protein 47g*

Baby beets

# Barley risotto, caramelized baby beets and grilled pork filet

GLOBE

2 pork filets, about 1 lb (450 g) each

Salt and freshly ground black pepper

MARINADE:

1 head garlic, coarsely chopped

1 red pepper, coarsely chopped

1 red onion, coarsely chopped

4 sprigs of coriander

1 cup (250 ml) olive oil

BEETS:

12 baby golden beets, or striped

Pinch dried rosemary, or thyme or marjoram

3 tbsp (45 ml) honey

BARLEY RISOTTO:

1 tsp (5 ml) canola oil

½ onion, finely chopped

2 cups (500 ml) uncooked barley

3 cups (750 ml) vegetable stock

2 tbsp (30 ml) grated Parmesan

Chopped fresh basil, parsley and sage

The beets can be prepared a day in advance. Heat oven to 350°F (180°C). Season with rosemary, salt and pepper. Wrap in aluminum foil and cook for 40-50 minutes or until tender. Cool before placing in refrigerator overnight. Pierce the pork filets with a sharp knife in several places before marinating. In a large container or ziplock bag, combine marinade ingredients and add filets, covering well with marinade. Let sit for at least 6 hours or overnight.

To prepare meal, remove beets from the refrigerator and cut into quarters. In a heavy frying pan over high heat, sauté beets together with honey. Remove from heat when beets are glossy and caramelized. Prepare risotto while beets are caramelizing. Heat canola oil in frying pan over medium heat. Add onion and stir. Before onion begins to color, add barley. Cook 3-5 minutes, stirring occasionally. Introduce stock a little at a time, until the barley is just covered. Stir to prevent sticking. Keep adding stock and stirring until most of the stock has been absorbed. Barley should still be firm. Just before serving, stir in Parmesan, basil, parsley and sage.

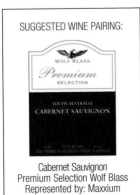

SUGGESTED WINE PAIRING:

WOLF BLASS

*Premium*

SELECTION

SOUTH AUSTRALIA

CABERNET SAUVIGNON

Cabernet Sauvignon
Premium Selection Wolf Blass
Represented by: Maxxium

Remove pork filets from marinade and season with salt and pepper. Heat heavy frying pan over high heat. Sear filets well on all sides. Lower heat and continue cooking, uncovered, until filets are done to your liking. Slice and arrange on serving plate around risotto topped with beets.

Substitution: Veal can be used instead of pork.

Serves 4

*Serving Size (730g), Calories 760, Total Fat 16g, Saturated Fat 4.5g, Cholesterol 115mg, Sodium 540mg, Total Carbohydrate 107g, Dietary Fiber 23g, Sugars 30g, Protein 52g*

# Mushroom and guinea fowl supreme

4 guinea fowl breasts

2 tbsp (30 ml) canola oil

1 cup (250 ml) chicken stock

7 oz (200 g) mushrooms, any type

1 shallot, minced

Salt and freshly ground black pepper

4 thyme sprigs for garnish

In a heavy frying pan heated to high, cook guinea fowl breasts in canola oil for about 10 minutes. Remove from pan and place on a warm plate. Deglaze pan with chicken stock, scraping up any brown bits. Over low heat, reduce stock until thickened. Season with salt and pepper.

Sauté mushrooms in same pan over high heat. Add shallots and sauté a few minutes more. To serve, place each guinea fowl breast on a plate and top with mushroom-shallot mixture. Drizzle with pan sauce and garnish with fresh thyme.

Suggested side dish: steamed green vegetables.

Serves 4

*Serving Size (485g), Calories 560, Total Fat 19g, Saturated Fat 4.5g, Cholesterol 210mg, Sodium 290mg, Total Carbohydrate 3g, Dietary Fiber-less than 1g, Sugars 1g, Protein 90g*

SUGGESTED WINE PAIRING:

Bolgheri Superiore
Le Serre Nuove dell'Ornellaia
Represented by: Maxxium

# Desserts

# Wild berry martini with yogurt, basil and orange zest

4 oz (115 g) strawberries, quartered

4 oz (115 g) raspberries

4 oz (115 g) blackberries

4 oz (115 g) blueberries

Zest and juice of 1 orange

Zest of ½ lemon

¾ oz (20 g) fresh basil, thinly sliced

1 oz (30 g) sugar

4 oz (115 g) low-fat plain yogurt

Sprig of mint for garnish

Place berries in bowl with orange zest, lemon zest, basil and sugar. Toss gently. Allow to marinate for 10 minutes. Divide berry mixture between 4 martini glasses and drizzle with orange juice. Top with dollop of yogurt and garnish with mint sprig.

Substitution: Mascarpone cheese may be substituted for the yogurt, but it will increase the fat and calorie content.

Serves 4

*Serving Size (170g), Calories 110, Total Fat 1g, Saturated Fat 0g, Cholesterol 0mg, Sodium 20mg,*
*Total Carbohydrate 24g, Dietary Fiber 5g, Sugars 18g, Protein 3g*

blackberries
blueberries
raspberries

# Pears in wine with caramel

2 cups (500 ml) red wine

5½ oz (155 g) sugar

¾ cup (190 ml) water

1 cinnamon stick

1 star anise

1 tsp (5 ml) whole peppercorns

3 grains whole cardamom

4 ripe pears


VANILLA YOGURT:

1 cup (250 ml) plain yogurt

2 tbsp (30 ml) honey

Beans from ½ vanilla pod
(see note)

Preparations for the vanilla yogurt must begin a day in advance. Place the plain yogurt in a coffee filter the night before and allow it to drain into a bowl overnight. The following day, discard the liquid and pour the thickened yogurt into a small bowl. Add the honey and vanilla and mix well.

In a medium-size pot over medium heat, warm the red wine, sugar, water and spices. Meanwhile, peel each pear, keeping the stem intact. Working up from the bottom, use a melon baller to remove the seeds and tough middle section. Add pears to wine mixture and simmer, uncovered, until tender when poked with a fork. Remove pot from heat and allow to cool.

Set pears aside and pass syrup through a sieve to remove spices. Return ½ cup (125 ml) of the syrup to the pot to make caramel. Place remaining syrup in a bowl and add cooked pears until time to serve. Make caramel by reducing the syrup over low heat until thick enough to coat the back of a spoon. To serve, smear caramel in the center of each plate as a base for the pear. Place pear on caramel and drizzle with syrup. Decorate the plate with caramel and top with a dollop of yogurt.

Note: To remove the vanilla beans, scrape the inside of the pod with a knife. If you prepare this dessert a few days in advance, the spices must be removed before refrigeration.

Serves 4

*Serving Size (395g), Calories 410, Total Fat 2g, Saturated Fat 0.5g, Cholesterol 5mg, Sodium 50mg, Total Carbohydrate 79g, Dietary Fiber 4g, Sugars 67g, Protein 4g*

SUGGESTED WINE PAIRING:

Taylor Fladgate
First Estate Reserve Port
Represented by: Whitehall Agencies

# Cinnamon stick

# Nougat, figs, almonds and tomato compote

LE CLUB
CHASSE
et PÊCHE

## NOUGAT

3 oz (85 g) water

1 cup (250 ml) sugar

⅓ cup (75 ml) honey

6 large egg whites

5 cups (1.25 l) 35% cream

12 dried figs, chopped

2 tbsp (30 ml) chopped almonds

2 tbsp (30 ml) chopped pistachios

3 tbsp (45 ml) chopped marinated ginger

1 cup (250 ml) orange zest confit for garnish
*(see note below)*

## TOMATO COMPOTE:

6.6 lbs (3 kg) orange or red cherry tomatoes

12 cups (3 l) water for boiling

4½ cups (1 kg) sugar

½ cup (125 ml) honey

1 vanilla bean

Pinch salt

To make nougat, combine water, sugar and honey in a small pot and heat to 250°F (120°C). Meanwhile, beat egg whites in a bowl until firm. When honey mixture is ready, quickly pour into egg white mixture. Beat until it regains its firmness. In a separate bowl, whip cream until almost firm. Stir in figs, almonds, pistachios and ginger. Gently fold into egg white mixture.

Cut parchment paper to fit a baking sheet. One spoonful at a time, transfer mixture to parchment paper, pressing each mound gently into an almond shape. Put sheet in freezer. Frozen nougat may be kept in freezer in an airtight container for several months.

Prepare tomato compote by making 2 small perpendicular cuts across the top of each tomato. Blanch tomatoes in salted water for no more than 10 seconds. Cool down in ice bath. When cool, remove skin. In large pot, bring water, sugar, honey and vanilla bean to a boil. Add tomatoes and simmer for 20 minutes. Remove tomatoes. Return sugar-honey mixture to low heat and reduce by half. Remove from heat and cool. Once cooled, add tomatoes. To serve, place frozen nougat in center of plate accompanied by tomatoes in reduction. Garnish with orange zest confit, if desired.

Note: See page 36 for the recipe for lemon zest confit. Substitute oranges for lemons.

Serves 36

*Nougat: Serving Size (56g), Calories 170, Total Fat 13g, Saturated Fat 8g, Cholesterol 45mg, Sodium 35mg, Total Carbohydrate 13g, Dietary Fiber-less than 1g, Sugars 12g, Protein 2g*
*Tomato Compote: Serving Size (30g), Calories 35, Total Fat 0g, Saturated Fat 0g, Cholesterol 0mg, Sodium 0mg, Total Carbohydrate 9g, Dietary Fiber 0g, Sugars 9g, Protein 0g*

SUGGESTED WINE PAIRING:

Ben Ryé
PASSITO DI PANTELLERIA

DONNAFUGATA

Passito di Panteleria
BEN RYÉ Donnafugata
Represented by: Maxxium

# Banana berry yogurt parfait

1 cup (250 ml) blueberries

½ cup (125 ml) strawberries

½ cup (125 ml) blackberries

1 tbsp (15 ml) icing sugar

1 tsp (5 ml) lemon juice

3 cups (750 ml) banana or vanilla yogurt

Whipped cream (optional)

4 cookies (optional)


STREUSEL:

½ cup (125 ml) all-purpose flour

⅓ cup (75 ml) brown sugar

⅓ cup (75 ml) white sugar

2 tbsp (30 ml) rolled oats

½ cup (125 ml) plus 2 tbsp (30 ml) butter, chilled and cubed

¼ cup (65 ml) banana chips, crushed

Heat oven to 350°F (180°C). Prepare streusel by mixing together brown and white sugars, flour and rolled oats in a food processor. Add butter and pulse until well combined. Spread mixture out on a baking sheet and bake until golden, about 10 minutes. While baking, stir every 2-3 minutes to break apart large chunks. Remove from oven and let cool. Mix in banana chips.

Before assembling parfaits, toss berries in icing sugar and lemon juice to coat. In each parfait cup, layer yogurt first, then berries followed by streusel. Leave 1 inch (2.5 cm) of space below glass rim. Serve with dollop of whipped cream and garnish with cookie, if desired.

Substitution: Macadamia nuts can be used instead of banana chips.

Serves 10

*Serving Size (170g), Calories 380, Total Fat 20g, Saturated Fat 13g, Cholesterol 45mg, Sodium 50mg, Total Carbohydrate 47g, Dietary Fiber 3g, Sugars 36g, Protein 4g*

Brownies

# Brownies

4 oz (115 g) butter

4 oz (115 g) 64% dark chocolate

2 eggs

6 oz (170 g) sugar

½ cup (125 ml) flour

¼ cup (65 ml) cocoa powder

½ cup (125 ml) white chocolate chips

½ cup (125 ml) milk chocolate chips

Heat oven to 350°F (180°C). Using a double boiler or microwave, melt butter and dark chocolate together. In a medium-size bowl, whip eggs and sugar together until creamy. Fold in butter-chocolate mixture. Sift flour and cocoa powder together and add to butter-chocolate mixture, folding gently. Fold in white and milk chocolate chips. Pour into greased 9x9" (23x23 cm) pan and cook for 35-40 minutes. When cool, cut into squares and serve.

Makes 16

*Serving Size (44g), Calories 200, Total Fat 11g, Saturated Fat 7g, Cholesterol 30mg, Sodium 85mg, Total Carbohydrate 25g, Dietary Fiber 1g, Sugars 17g, Protein 2g*

SUGGESTED WINE PAIRING:

Passito di Pantelleria d.o.c.
Pellegrino
Offered by: Italvine

# Giboulée de griottes

**cuisine inspirée**

**YOGURT TOPPING:**

2 cups (500 ml) plain or 2% yogurt

½ cup (125 ml) water

½ cup (125 ml) sugar

**CHERRIES:**

1 tsp (5 ml) butter

1 tsp (5 ml) olive oil

2 tbsp (30 ml) brown sugar

1 tsp (5 ml) ground cinnamon

2 tsp (10 ml) white vinegar

8 oz (225 g) cherries

Pinch white pepper

**EGG WHITE SORBET:**

5 egg whites

4 tbsp (60 ml) sugar

⅓ cup (75 ml) ground walnuts

**CRUMBLE:**

½ cup (125 ml) flour

½ cup (125 ml) sugar

½ cup (125 ml) crushed nuts, any kind

¼ tsp (1 ml) Szechuan pepper

½ cup (125 ml) butter

YOGURT TOPPING: In a medium-size bowl, mix ingredients together until well incorporated and place in freezer, covered, for 6 hours, stirring well every 2 hours. (This can also be made in an ice cream machine.)

CHERRIES: Cook butter, olive oil, brown sugar and cinnamon in a medium-size pot on low heat until lightly caramelized, stirring occasionally. Add vinegar, cherries and pepper and cook slowly, covered, for 1 hour or until cherries are lightly candied. Transfer to container and refrigerate.

EGG WHITE SORBET: In a medium-size bowl, beat egg whites until soft peaks form. Add sugar and continue to beat until stiff peaks form. Gently fold in walnuts. Divide meringue among 2-inch-high (5 cm) ramekins and microwave on high for 30 seconds. Place in refrigerator until cold.

CRUMBLE: Heat oven to 300°F (150°C). In a medium-size bowl, stir together flour, sugar, nuts, pepper and butter. Divide into small square pieces, place on cookie sheet and bake for 10 minutes. Cool.

TO ASSEMBLE: Scoop egg white sorbet onto plate, cover with crumble, top with yogurt and decorate with cherries.

Serves 20 to 30

*Serving Size (47g), Calories 110, Total Fat 6g, Saturated Fat 2g, Cholesterol 10mg, Sodium 50mg, Total Carbohydrate 13g, Dietary Fiber 0g, Sugars 10g, Protein 2g*

# Figue confite with muscat

8 bunches arugula

### FIGUE CONFITE:

4 tsp (20 ml) brown sugar

8 fresh figs, halved

5 tbsp (75 ml) plus 1 tsp (5 ml) Serra cheese

Pinch chopped rosemary

Honey for drizzling

### CONFITURE OF BLACKBERRIES AND MUSCAT:

1 cup (250 ml) red wine vinegar

¼ cup (65 ml) white sugar

1 cup (250 ml) fresh blackberries

1 cup (250 ml) Muscat wine

To prepare *figue confite*, heat oven to 350°F (180°C). Place brown sugar in a small oven-proof dish and top with whole figs. Cook for about 3 minutes. Remove from oven, slice figs in half and place 1 tsp (5 ml) cheese on each half. Sprinkle with pinch rosemary. Broil in oven until golden, about 30 seconds.

To prepare *confiture*, mix together red wine vinegar and sugar in a pot on high heat and bring to a boil. Reduce liquid by half. Add most of the blackberries and Muscat. Reduce heat to low and cook until liquid has thickened, then pass through a sieve. Return *confiture* to the pot, add the last few blackberries and bring to a boil. Remove from heat. To serve, spread out arugula on a plate. Arrange stuffed figs on top and drizzle with honey. Decorate the plate with the *confiture*.

Serves 8

*Serving Size (165g), Calories 150, Total Fat 1.5g, Saturated Fat 1g, Cholesterol 5mg, Sodium 80mg, Total Carbohydrate 27g, Dietary Fiber 3g, Sugars 23g, Protein 2g*

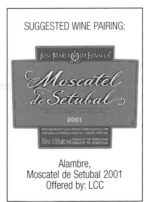

SUGGESTED WINE PAIRING:

Alambre,
Moscatel de Setubal 2001
Offered by: LCC

# Light chocolate panacotta

3 gelatin sheets

1⅔ cups (400 ml) 1% milk

4 oz (115 g) 70% chocolate, chopped

2 tsp (10 ml) honey

Dissolve gelatin sheets in a bit of cold water. In a pot on medium heat, warm milk just to boiling. Remove from heat. Add dissolved gelatin to milk and stir. In a separate bowl, pour warmed milk mixture onto chocolate pieces. Whisk in honey until well blended. Pour into 4 ramekins and refrigerate.

Serves 4

*Serving Size (149g), Calories 230, Total Fat 7g, Saturated Fat 5g, Cholesterol 5mg, Sodium 140mg, Total Carbohydrate 21g, Dietary Fiber 1g, Sugars 18g, Protein 23g*

honey
chocolate

SUGGESTED WINE PAIRING:

Taylor Fladgate
Late Bottled Vintage Port
Represented by: Whitehall Agencies

# Four by four

TOWNE
HALL

## CAKE:

1 lb (450 g) butter

2 cups (500 ml) sugar

10 eggs

2 tbsp (30 ml) vanilla

2 cups (500 ml) flour

1 tbsp (15 ml) baking powder

1 cup (250 ml) marmalade

## SYRUP:

2 cups (500 ml) water

1½ cups (375 ml) sugar

1 tsp (5 ml) lemon juice

## Chocolate mousse

½ lb (225 g) 70% dark chocolate

2 cups (500 ml) 35% cream

---

Heat oven to 350°F (180°C). In a large bowl, cream together butter and sugar until fluffy. Add eggs and vanilla and continue beating. In a separate bowl, combine flour and baking powder. Slowly mix dry ingredients into egg mixture. Fold in marmalade. Pour ingredients into greased 13x9-inch (35x25 cm) baking pan and bake for 30-35 minutes.

To make syrup, bring all ingredients to a boil in a pot. Stir until sugar has dissolved. Remove from heat. Pour warm syrup over warm cake in pan. Let cool and serve.

Melt chocolate in double boiler or microwave. Cool. Whip cream. Add one third of the whipped cream to chocolate, whisking vigorously. Gently fold in remaining whipped cream. Refrigerate. Can be served as a topping for the four by four.

Option: For a slightly stronger orange flavor, add 4 tbsp (60 ml) Grand Marnier to syrup just prior to removing from heat.

Serves 20 to 24

*Serving Size (106g), Calories 440, Total Fat 25g, Saturated Fat 15g, Cholesterol 155mg, Sodium 110mg, Total Carbohydrate 51g, Dietary Fiber 0g, Sugars 40g, Protein 4g*

SUGGESTED WINE PAIRING:

Muscat de Panteleria
KABIR Donnafugata
Represented by: Maxxium

# Karithopita crème brûlée

**CAKE:**

½ cup (125 ml) plus 2 tbsp (30 ml) all-purpose flour

½ tsp (2 ml) baking powder

1 tsp (5 ml) cinnamon

2 tbsp (30 ml) cocoa powder

Pinch salt

½ cup (125 ml) plus 2 tbsp (30 ml) chopped walnuts

10 eggs, separated

10 tbsp (150 ml) sugar

**SYRUP:**

1 cup (250 ml) white sugar

1 cup (250 ml) water

1 tbsp (15 ml) cocoa powder

**CRÈME BRÛLÉE:**

3 cups (750 ml) 35% cream

½ cup (125 ml) homogenized milk

Zest of 1 orange

¾ cup (175 ml) white sugar, divided

8 egg yolks

3 tbsp (45 ml) Grand Marnier

White sugar for topping

Heat oven to 350°F (180°C). In a bowl, sift together flour, baking powder, cinnamon, cocoa powder and salt. Mix in chopped walnuts. Beat 10 egg yolks with 5 tbsp (75 ml) sugar until color has whitened. Set aside.

To prepare syrup, bring sugar and water to a boil. Add cocoa and boil again. Remove from heat. In a separate bowl, beat 10 egg whites with remaining sugar. Stop beating just before eggs form a soft meringue. Pour egg yolk mixture into bowl with flour mixture. Spoon one quarter of egg white mixture onto egg yolk-flour mixture and fold in. Add remaining egg white mixture and continue to fold in.

Fill 3-inch-wide (7.5 cm) metal ring molds half full with batter. Bake for 25 minutes. Remove from oven and brush tops with warm syrup. Let cool. Reduce oven to 250°F (125°C).

To prepare crème brûlée, whisk cream, milk, zest and half the sugar in a pot and bring to a boil. Remove from heat. Beat egg yolks with remaining sugar until whitened. Place 1 ladle of warm cream mixture into cold egg yolk mixture and stir well. When combined, add remaining cream mixture and continue to stir. Add Grand Marnier and incorporate well.

Spoon three quarters of an inch of crème brûlée mixture onto each cake. Bake for 45-60 minutes. Do not overcook. Crème brûlée will be jiggly when removed from oven. Allow to cool, then refrigerate. Just before serving, sprinkle sugar on top of cakes and place under broiler or torch with baking tool until sugar bubbles golden-brown.

Serves 8 to 10

*Serving Size (212g), Calories 640, Total Fat 41g, Saturated Fat 20g, Cholesterol 480mg, Sodium 160mg, Total Carbohydrate 59g, Dietary Fiber 1g, Sugars 50g, Protein 13g*

SUGGESTED WINE PAIRING:

Taylor Fladgate 20 Year Old
Tawny Port
Represented by: Whitehall Agencies

# White chocolate cheesecake

MONTREAL BREAD COMPANY

1 cup (250 ml) 35% cream

1 tsp (5 ml) vanilla

2 cups (500 ml) cream cheese, at room temperature

12 packets low-calorie sweetener

2 cups (500 ml) 4% fine-texture cottage cheese

1½ cups (375 ml) chopped white chocolate

Graham crackers, crushed

Fresh berries for garnish

Dark chocolate, melted

In a small bowl, lightly beat cream with an electric mixer until slightly thickened. Beat in vanilla. In a large bowl, beat cream cheese and sweetener until smooth. Add cottage cheese and beat until combined.

Melt white chocolate in a double boiler or microwave. Remove from heat. Spoon a small amount of cream cheese mixture into melted chocolate. Stir gently to combine. Pour cream cheese-and-chocolate mixture into remaining cream cheese mixture and fold together. Gently fold in cream.

Pat a thin layer of crushed graham crackers into the bottom of individual serving dishes. Pour mixture on top. Refrigerate for 1 day. Serve topped with fresh berries and a drizzle of melted chocolate.

Serves 8 to 10

*Serving Size (152g), Calories 440, Total Fat 33g, Saturated Fat 20g, Cholesterol 85mg, Sodium 350mg, Total Carbohydrate 29g, Dietary Fiber 2g, Sugars 10g, Protein 10g*

berries & chocolate

SUGGESTED WINE PAIRING:

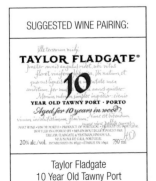

TAYLOR FLADGATE
10
YEAR OLD TAWNY PORT · PORTO
Aged for 10 years in wood

20% alc./vol.    750 ml

Taylor Fladgate
10 Year Old Tawny Port
Represented by: Whitehall Agencies

# Insalata di fragole
## con aceto balsamico
# Strawberry and balsamic salad

2 cups (500 ml) fresh strawberries cut into quarters

2 tbsp (30 ml) aged balsamic vinegar

1 tbsp (15 ml) freshly squeezed lemon juice

3½ tbsp (52 ml) white sugar

1 tbsp (15 ml) Passito di Pantelleria Italian dessert wine (optional)

Pepper to taste

Mint leaves for garnish

Place strawberries in a bowl. Add vinegar, lemon juice, sugar and wine, if using. Stir gently to combine. Cover and let sit at room temperature for about 1 hour. Divide among 6 serving cups and sprinkle with pepper. Garnish each serving with mint leaves.

Serves 6

*Serving Size (68g), Calories 50, Total Fat 0g, Saturated Fat 0g, Cholesterol 0mg, Sodium 0mg, Total Carbohydrate 12g, Dietary Fiber 1g, Sugars 11g, Protein 0g*

SUGGESTED WINE PAIRING:

Passito di Panteleria BEN RYÉ
Donnafugata
Represented by: Maxxium

Mint&lemon

1. **40 Westt & Towne Hall:** Executive Chef Stefanos Hinoporos 2. **40 Westt:** Chef Gerson Lemus 3. **Pintxo:** Chef Alonso Ortiz Avila 4. **Fairmount Tremblant:** Executive Chef Daniel Tobien 5. **Fairmount Tremblant:** Sous-Chef Ken Coderre 6. **Ferreira:** Marino Tavares 7. **Queue de Cheval:** Chief Butcher Gavino D'iglio 8. **Queue de Cheval:** Executive Chef Stéphane Dumas 9. **Queue de Cheval:** Head Chef Michael Cologgi 10. **Primo & Secondo:** Chef Roberto Stabile 11. **Il Mulino:** Executive Chef Tony Derose 12. **Il Mulino:** Pastry Chef Annie Laliberté 13. **Il Mulino:** Chef Gabriel Berlinguet 14. **Il Mulino:** Chef David Zaccardi 15. **La Louisiane:** Chef Sean Hayes 16. **Le Club Chasse et Pêche:** Pastry Chef Masami Waki 17. **Le Club Chasse et Pêche:** Chef François Cadieux 18. **Le Club Chasse et Pêche:** Head Chef Claude Pelletier 19. **Prima Luna:** Assistant Chef Jian Carlo Farella 20. **Prima Luna:** Assistant Chef Orazio Conetta 21. **Prima Luna:** Executive Chef Andrea Dell'Orefice 22. **Milos:** Chef George Spiliadis 23. **Le Gourmand:** Chef Michael Oliphant 24. **Lucca:** Chef Adelino Domingues 25. **Maestro S.V.P.:** Chef Yves Therrien 26. **Trinity:** Chef John Zoumis 27. **Mount Stephen Club:** Chef Frank Barbusci 28. **Towne Hall:** Sous-Chef Angelo Baggio 29. **Towne Hall:** Pastry Chef Spyros Samidas 30. **Le Renoir:** Chef Deff Haupt 31. **Le Renoir:** Sous-Chef Julien Montagne 32. **Le Renoir:** Pastry Chef Pascal Thouvenot 33. **YoYo:** Chef Bernard-Simon Catafard 34. **Taverne sur le Square:** Chef Stephen Leslie 35. **Vino Rosso:** Chef Bruno Varano 36. **Vino Rosso:** Chef Nick DeRubertis

## 40 Westt 2305 Trans-Canada Highway, Pointe-Claire 514.428.9378

## Bice 1504 Sherbrooke Street West, Montreal 514.937.6009

## Cavalli 2040 Peel Street, Montreal 514.843.5100

## Fairmount Tremblant 3045 Chapelle Road, Mont Tremblant 819.681.7603

## Ferreira Café 1446 Peel Street, Montreal 514.848.0988

## Globe 3455 St-Laurent Boulevard, Montreal 514.284.3823

## Il Cortile 1442 Sherbrooke Street West, Montreal 514.843.8230

## Il Mulino 236 St-Zotique Street East, Montreal 514.273.5776

## La Louisiane 5850 Sherbrooke Street West, Montreal 514.369.3073

## Le Club Chasse et Pêche 423 St-Claude Street, Montreal 514.861.1112

## Le Gourmand 42 Ste-Anne Avenue, Pointe-Claire 514.695.9077

## Le Piment Rouge 1170 Peel Street, Montreal 514.866.7816

## Le Renoir (Sofitel Hotel) 1155 Sherbrooke Street West, Montreal 514.788.3038

## Lucca 12 Dante Street, Montreal 514.278.6502

The
making
of the
book

# Linguine with Leeks and Clams *(Linguine con Porri e Vongole Veraci)*

## Ingredients

2 pounds clams

3 medium leeks

2 cups white wine

2 cloves garlic

1/4 cup extra virgin olive oil

1 bay leaf

2 tablespoons butter

4 tablespoons Italian parsley, chopped

Sea salt to taste

Freshly ground black pepper to taste

1 box (500 grams) **BARILLA** Linguine

**SOAK** the clams in water for one hour with sea salt. Rinse well after soaking. **BRING** a large pot of water to a boil.

**CHOP** the garlic thinly and sauté in a skillet with the olive oil. **ADD** the clams, bay leaf and wine. Cover and cook until the shells open. Discard half of the shells and filter the juices. **MELT** butter in a separate pan; add leeks and sweat them for 3-4 minutes. Adjust with salt and black pepper. **ADD** the leeks to the skillet with the clams and simmer for one minute. **COOK** pasta two minutes less than the recommended cooking time on the package. Drain, saving a small amount of the cooking water. **TOSS** hot pasta with the sauce, adding pasta cooking water if sauce becomes too dry. Finish with chopped parsley.

*Sager Food Products is the Exclusive Importer of Barilla pasta. For more recipes, please visit www.barillaus.com*

LES PRODUITS ALIMENTAIRES
Sager
FOOD PRODUCTS

# THERE ARE MANY PENNE
# BUT THERE IS ONLY ONE DE CECCO.

Since 1887, De Cecco has been producing superior quality pasta which has won worldwide recognition from pasta lovers and celebrated chefs for its exceptional taste and cooking consistency.

You can rest assured that in the blue box there is delicious, premium-quality pasta imported from Italy.

## DE CECCO®

"There is only one De Cecco"

www.dececco.it
For information: 1-888-IDFOODS
www.idfoods.com

**Saputo**
www.saputo.com

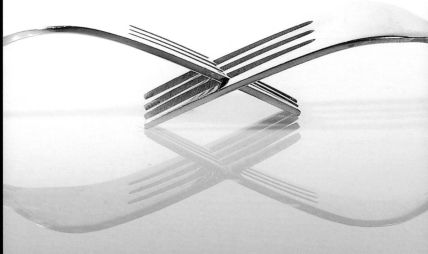
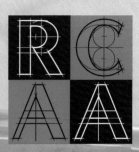

Centre universitaire de santé McGill

McGill University Health Centre

Les meilleurs soins pour la vie
The Best Care for Life

# COMPLIMENTS OF

**MONIT**

## ALEX KOTLER
## &
## BARRY KOTLER

EILEEN
FISHER

IN PROUD SUPPORT OF
MUHC'S WOMEN'S HEALTH MISSION

# CONSORTIUM D'ENTREPRISES

Planification - Organisation
Supervision - Logistique
Gestion de projets et de relocalisation
Déménagement

  ET

**CFG GESTIONNAIRE
EN RELOCALISATION**
Courtiers en environnement de bureau
8572, boul. Pie-IX
Montréal, Québec
H1Z 4G2
Tél. : 514-729-5301
Fax. : 514-322-9920

**PROJEXPACE Inc.**
Spécialiste en relocalisation
5150, rue Quevillon
St-Hubert, Québec
J3Y 2V4
Tél. : 450-656-5998
Fax. : 450-656-8761

**Nous sommes fiers de participer
à la mission Santé des femmes du CUSM**

Jean Sébastien Giguère
President

850 Marshall Street
Laval (Quebec) H7S 1K1
Tel.: 450–667–6877, ext. 27
Fax: 450–667–4277
Cell.: 514–219–9313
jeansebastien.giguere@mofax.ca

mofax@mofax.ca
R.B.Q. 1117-5635-79

**mofax**
ÉLECTRIQUE
A TRADITION OF QUALITY
SINCE **1939**

We are happy to be partners with the MUHC and to contribute to the success of the Women's Health Mission.

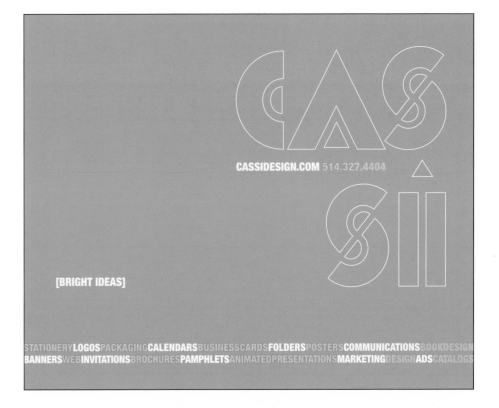

CASSIDESIGN.COM 514.327.4404

[BRIGHT IDEAS]

STATIONERY LOGOS PACKAGING CALENDARS BUSINESSCARDS FOLDERS POSTERS COMMUNICATIONS BOOKDESIGN BANNERS WEB INVITATIONS BROCHURES PAMPHLETS ANIMATEDPRESENTATIONS MARKETING DESIGN ADS CATALOGS

TECSULT

N. SANI CIE LTÉE

Westcliff Group

SITE ALPHA INC.

MAIN (1996)
Matériaux de Plomberie
et Chauffage Inc.

THE COLA FAMILY

B. Kaplan Construction Inc.

Claridge Inc.

To my uncle, Mehmet Yavuz, who introduced me to
photography and inspired me to become a photographer
Fahri Yavuz, photographer

ROCHE Ltée, Groupe-Conseil

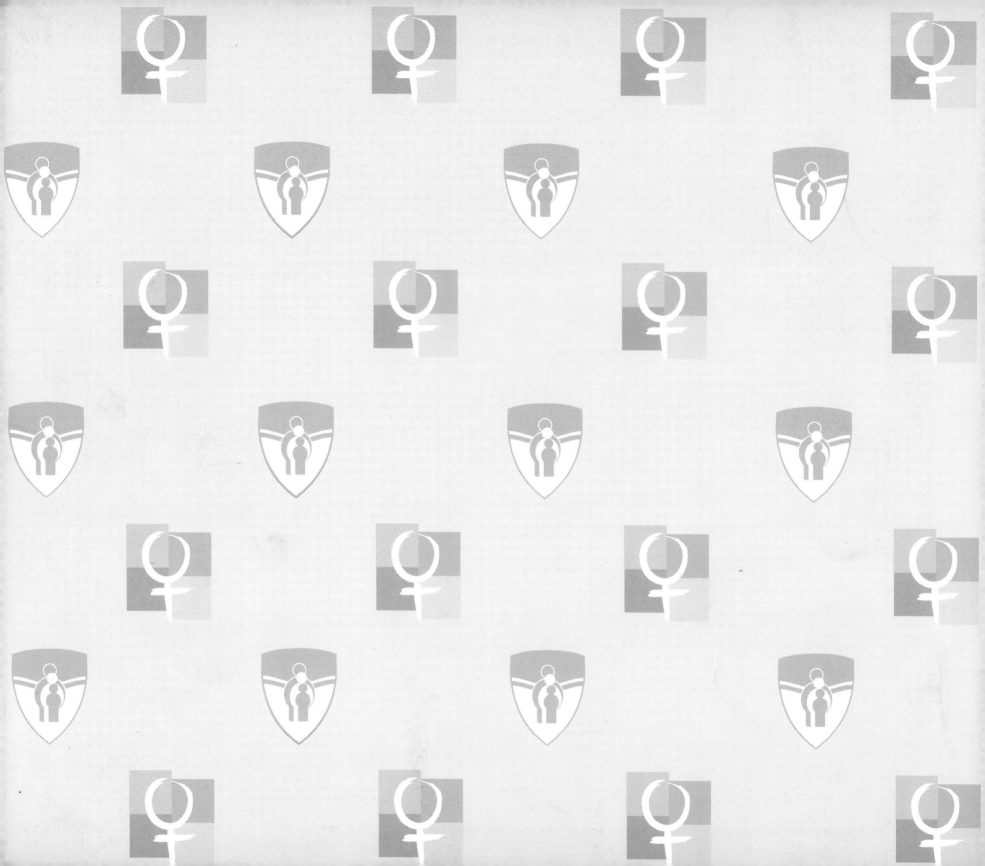